MY SPACE ON EARTH

Renee
May your day ahead be perfect in every way.
Love,
Gayle
2006

My Space On Earth

Irene Florence Paddock Ivory

IVORY HOUSE PUBLISHING

Ivory House Publishing
11828 Parkview Ct SW
Tumwater, WA 98512
(360) 754-7879

ISBN-10: 0-9787090-0-4
ISBN-13: 978-0-9787090-0-6
Library of Congress Control Number: 2006932618

I dedicate my life story to my dearest children.

Contents

Photographs

ACKNOWLEDGMENT

I am indebted to my daughter Gayle Ivory Strom
who has dedicated hundreds of hours deciphering, compiling,
typing, editing, proof reading and completing this project.

POEM BY IRENE PADDOCK

Some where out yonder
In that dearer life above
We shall understand each other
In the blessed light of love

When the storm clouds are lifted
and a bright light from the rugged shore
Guides our footsteps homeward
Our cares and troubles will be oe'r

The things that we most long for
Always seem so far away
And the love for which we labored
Was not ours at close of day

Life is but a lesson
Love can come to those who really care
Guide your loving thoughts homeward
Many will be there to share

(No date)

Pedigree Chart for Irene Florence PADDOCK

Page

No. 1 on this chart is the same as no. 1 on chart no. 1

Chart no.

1 **Irene Florence PADDOCK [4]**
b. 1 Jul 1912
p. Eureka, Humboldt, CA
m. 14 Dec 1938 [2]
p. Reno, Washoe, NV
d. 23 Oct 2003
p. Othello, Adams Co., WA
sp. Royal Andrew IVORY [3]

2 **Garfield Lincoln PADDOCK [9]**
b. 25 Jun 1882
p. Freeland Twp., Lac Qui Parle, MN
m. 20 Oct 1906 [7]
p. Eureka, Humboldt, CA
d. 3 Nov 1928
p. Union Labor Hosp., Eureka, Humboldt, CA

3 **Ida Belle FULMORE [10]**
b. 21 Jul 1888
p. Wakefield, Gogebic, MI
d. 30 Mar 1972
p. Eureka, Humboldt, CA

4 **William Cornell PADDOCK [46]**
b. 9 Dec 1839
p. Genoa, Dekalb, IL
m. 13 Jan 1878 [32]
p. Sumner, Fillmore, MN
d. 26 Sep 1924
p. Trinidad, Humboldt, CA

5 **Loena Roxana LASELL [45]**
b. 28 May 1855
p. Morgan, Orleans, VT
d. 1 Sep 1941
p. Trinidad, Humboldt, CA

6 **Charles FULMORE [52]**
b. Abt 1858
p. Nova Scotia, Canada
m. [35]
p.
d.
p.

7 **Amelia Frances BOWDEN [51]**
b. 24 May 1867
p. Cornwall, England
d. 22 Jun 1944
p. Imola , Napa, CA

8 **William Cornell PADDOCK [48]**
b. 1 Jun 1794-1795
p. Sullivan Co. NY
m. 8 Jul 1824-1825 [33]
p.
d. 12 May 1887
p. Caledonia, MN

9 **Almira DOCETT [47]**
b. 28 Apr 1802
p. Sullivan Co, NY
d. 14 Sep 1877
p. Caledonia, MN

10 **Zaro Dana LASELL [50]**
b. 20 Sep 1831
p. Dudswell Que
m. 4 Jul 1854 [34]
p. West Charleston VT
d. 1911
p. Waubay, Day Co., SD

11 **Roxana Moon LUND [49]**
b. 9 Aug 1833
p. Ellenburg, NY
d. 16 Apr 1900
p. Waubay, Day Co., SD

12 **Alexander J. FULMORE [740]**
b. 9 Sep 1812
p. Five Islands, Colchester, Nova Scotia, Canada
m. 1846 [472]
p. Five Islands, Colchester, Nova Scotia
d. 30 Aug 1884
p. Nova Scotia, Canada

13 **Mary MILLER [741]**
b. Abt 1822
p. Nova Scotia, Canada
d. 30 Aug 1884
p. Folly Lake, Colchester, Nova Scotia?

14 **William Henry BOWDEN [53]**
b. 4 Jul 1830
p. Eng.
m. [36]
p.
d.
p.

15 **Amelia FRANCIS [1211]**
b. 6 Jul 1831
p. Eng.
d.
p.

16 **Capt. Jonathon PADDOCK [166]**
b. Jun 1765
d. After 1832

17 **Hannah TAYLOR [167]**
b.
d.

18 **Peter Barzeal DOCETT [689]**
b.
d.

19 **Unnamed [2246]**
b.
d.

20 **Dr. Thomas Dana LASELL [169]**
b. 11 Nov 1770
d. 8 Jun 1854

21 **Mary Elizabeth Ann CARGILL [170]**
b. 30 Dec 1797
d. 9 Apr 1879

22 **Silas LUND [179]**
b. 1 May 1807
d. 25 Oct 1882

23 **Charity DARLING [3447]**
b. After 1802
d.

24 **Andrew William FULMORE [742]**
b. 14 Feb 1784
d. 17 May 1872

25 **Margaret VANCE [743]**
b. 1791
d. 22 Nov 1836

26
b.
d.

27
b.
d.

28 **William H BOWDEN [1212]**
b.
d.

29
b.
d.

30
b.
d.

31
b.
d.

Produced by Legacy on 11 Jun 2

MY SPACE ON EARTH

by **Irene Paddock Ivory**
as told to her daughter, **Gayle Strom**

During my lifetime I have left my footprints on such an insignificant small part of this earth, yet I have tried to be a part of the design of the universe by fulfilling my part as best as my abilities allowed. There is a part of me that goes back to the beginning of human life. That part has come down from generation to generation, and I extend that part of me to my children and they have passed it on to their children which gives my life a continuity that will not end. I have a deep love and compassion for all those ancestors who are a part of me and a part of what I am. I have taken their space on earth. While here I have tried to fulfill a part of their dreams as well as mine.

My space on earth began July 1, 1912 in a little northern town located in Northern California. Someone gave it the name of Eureka and it was situated in Humboldt County. In it's beginning it was nestled among the giant redwood trees growing around the waters of Humboldt Bay. The bay protected the town from the waters of the mighty Pacific Ocean. The splendor of this beautiful part of our earth was an outstanding place to begin my journey on earth. My family's beginning began when my Father married my Mother on October 18, 1906 in Eureka, California. My sister, Lucille Rebecca was born January 30, 1908. My brother Sterling Fillmore was born April 11, 1910, and my brother William Cornell Paddock was born February 10, 1914. Lucille was born in a nursing home called The Gaynor Nursing Home. Sterling, Cornell and I were born at home in Eureka. Doctor Ottmer was our family doctor so he attended my mother during delivery.

Before going on with my story I must say something about this most wonderful doctor. Dr. Ottmer was a happy, jolly man. He was about six feet tall, heavy set and especially kind to all of his little patients. He had a brown mustache that would twitch up at the corners when he tipped his head back to laugh. He laughed a great deal and his laughter seemed to fill every corner of the room. He was our family doctor and we loved him and he loved us. Dr. Ottmer didn't have any children of his own so he lavished his affection on his sick little patients. His vacations were spent hunting for big game and many of these animals were stuffed and some made into rugs. When ever I had to go to his office the first thing that I did when entering was to lay down on the white polar bear skin. His hunting trips took him to Africa, South America, and Alaska, so his trophies consisted of many wild animal species. My first visit to his office was scary. Having the eyes of so many animals staring at me was frightening but Dr. Ottmer held me in his arms and let me feel the faces of the stuffed animals while telling me about each one in his kind gentle voice. When holding me I could smell the aromatic odor of a rich blend of tobacco that he smoked in a very large hand carved bowl pipe. Visiting this wonderful man's office was very exciting for me. Almost as exciting as going to the zoo.

Garfield Lincoln Paddock

While living in Eureka, my father, Garfield Lincoln Paddock worked for Buhners and Grunts department stores as a delivery man. Dad had two bay horses and a large wagon to carry out his duties. Anyone having a wagon and horses could usually find some kind of delivery work. Dad also did long shore work which involved loading and unloading ships. Our town like many coastal towns depended upon the shipping lanes to supply the people with many necessities.

We lived in Eureka until I was about 2 years old. Then we moved to Bridgeville where my Dad filed for a homestead. It was a very remote mountainous area about eighty miles from anywhere. Scrub oak, manzanita, and huge pepperwood trees dominated the terrain and afforded thick cover for wild animals such as cougar, bear, coyotes, raccoons, and all the other little animals like chipmunks and squirrels. It was a naturalists paradise and my brother Sterling and I were little naturalists. The birds, bees, butterflies and insects kept us busy the whole day long during the beautiful seasons of the year when the sun shone down on our amazing wonderful earth. Those years were so carefree, happy and filled with love even though we were virtually isolated from the rest of the human race. My mother, Ida Belle Fulmore Paddock, was the only one in our family who was unhappy with such remote living conditions. She was a very social type of person. She loved to entertain, go to dances, and have many people around to enliven the conversation. My mother was pregnant with my brother, Cornell, during this period of our lives.

Sterling and Irene Paddock

LIFE ON THE HOMESTEAD

Before moving us out to the homestead Dad constructed a small cabin. All the materials had to be hauled over narrow dirt roads by horse and wagon. It involved fifty miles of simply agonizing work for man and beast because of rutted roads and steep hills with overhanging bushes and limbs from trees slapping at your body as your team of horses plodded on. Many times Dad would have to get down from the high seat of the wagon and push while his hired man urged the team of horses to pull a little harder. Occasionally a wild animal would bound away through the underbrush and startle the horses. On one trip up the mountain a black bear walked out into the center of the road in front of the team and stood up on its hind legs which frightened the horses. Both of them reared up and started to plow through the bushes. Some of the lumber and supplies fell off the wagon. Dad grabbed the metal from around the seat of the wagon and managed to hang on. Dad always took a rifle along on his trips but didn't want to use it because a loud noise could frighten the horses and make the situation much worse. Dad and the hired man yelled and clapped their hands at the bear which was enough to send him scurrying across the road and into the bushes. They waited quietly while listening to the bear as he ran down the mountain side. Dad climbed down off the wagon and helped untangle the team, got them back on the road and restocked the supplies that had fallen off the wagon.

The day that Dad moved the family to the homestead was exciting for us. Mother and the three of us kids rode with Dad in the lead wagon. My Uncle

Marion Paddock followed with the supply wagon. A couple of days before our trip Mother baked bread, made a cake, and some cookies and the night before leaving she fried chicken and made a potato salad. These goodies would be eaten beside a mountain stream the next day. All of us were tired of riding in a cramped position and being jostled for about six hours so when we arrived at the Van Duzen river we were ready for food and exercise. I don't remember this trip too well as I was only little past 2 years of age but this was a regular stopping place for all of the trips that followed. As I grew older I remember falling into the river once. I was looking for minnows and slipped on the rocks getting my long dress and high topped shoes wet. Mom was really put out about this and scolded me. I got quite cold standing in the shade of the mountain and trees while Mom dug through the load on the wagon looking for a dry change of garments for me. I felt miserable and hated it. We always had an overnight stop, and sometimes if we got a late start from Eureka we would have to camp by the river overnight because traveling at night over that crooked dirt road was difficult. There were lots of redwood trees in the Van Duzen region. At night we slept on the ground and looked up at the stars through those towering giants.

Previous to our final move Dad had installed a wood cookstove and had cut some oak trees for wood so it would be ready for us when we arrived. He also had taken the beds and set them up so things were easier for all of us. Dad had left the hired man at the homestead while he came alone to Eureka to get us. The hired man killed a deer, a young spike buck so that we would have fresh meat for our dinner. Since it was early spring the meat kept well for several days. What meat wasn't eaten fresh was dried or cooked in stews or roasts. The meat of the young spike buck was tender and flavorful and they were very plentiful. The deer fed on acorns, grasses, and the tender shoots from the underbrush or shrubs.

I felt like I was in heaven when we lived on the homestead. Every day it seemed that nature provided us with something new and exciting. The beauty of everything filled my heart to overflowing. I felt bubbly and bursting with happiness as I explored and played in this part of God's world.

The cabin was small with only two rooms. One large room and one small room. The small room was as a bedroom for all of us children. Mom and Dad slept in the large family room which also served as the kitchen and dining area. The siding was made from redwood boards butted together as tightly as possible but there were cracks so the wind could blow through and this was the only protection that the cabin afforded us from the elements of the weather. Mother knew that something would have to be done about this problem so she pasted newspapers on the inside walls. Several layers of the newspapers helped to keep out the wind and cold and created a snugger, cozier feeling for all of us. She hung some pictures on the walls to brighten things up.

To prove-up on a homestead, a family had to build a house and clear the land as well as live on the land for a given period of time. Dad and the hired man cut the trees and used them for firewood. Since all the heating and cooking was done by wood burning stoves, it was necessary to have lots of wood cut and stacked ready for use. Much of the wood consisted of oak, manzanita, madrona, pepperwood and maple. These hardwoods burned well and were long lasting and they produced much heat. Dad would stoke the fire before going to bed at night which helped to ward off the chill while we slept. On very cold nights, Mom or Dad would get up and stoke the fire again.

Grandpa, William C. Paddock, spent that first summer on the homestead with us which was a special blessing for Mom. He kept a keen eye on me, Lucille, and Sterling too. Since I was a toddler it was necessary for someone to watch me rather closely. Mom and Dad were afraid that we might get lost if we wandered too far into the trees and bushes. Grandpa was a very entertaining person. He loved to sing for us and he had a very beautiful voice. He would hold me on his lap or knee and bounce me up and down and sing "Little Brown Jug" which delighted me. I think he learned many songs while he served as a soldier in the Civil War. These he sang to us. Grandpa was very handy with a pocket knife. He did a lot of whittling so kept Sterl entertained. He taught Sterl how to build figure four traps to catch small animals such as rabbits, squirrels, and birds. Another hobby of Grandpa's was to search for honey bee trees. Sterl usually tagged along after him while he was on a honey hunting excursion. Grandpa and Sterl kept the wood box full for Mom's cooking. Sterl wasn't very big being only 3 ½ years old, but he managed to carry several sticks of wood. Grandpa was as a very handsome old man. He had beautiful dark blue eyes, lots of snow white hair and a long white beard. He was a large man, a little over six feet tall and weighed 200 pounds. Very impressive to little children. I can never remember Grandpa being angry. He was always happy, cheerful and kind to everyone. This big kind gentle man had much influence on all of us children. Just having him there helped to drive away the loneliness for Mom, especially when Dad had to be away from home on a cattle buying trip.

One summer and winter my Uncle George Paddock stayed with us. He slept in a small shed that was about a half block away. He hated to sleep there alone so when he got ready to go to bed he would make a mad dash for the shed so he could get inside and close the door before some prowling animal might attack. There were many mountain lions all around our home and every night you could hear them yowling and screaming at each other. They often sounded like a woman or child screaming. Uncle George was about nineteen that year and had never lived in such wilderness. He slept inside the cabin during the winter months when it was cold and when the snow would cover everything with six or seven foot drifts. Our little cabin was much warmer when it was almost covered with snow.

Just before winter set in that first year on the homestead, Mom decided to fill the larger cracks in the boards on the outside of the house with rags. The boards were nailed vertically on the outside and when they shrunk there were some cracks about an inch wide. Many of our friends and town relatives had given us boxes of old clothes so Mom used some of these to chink the cracks. This made quite an improvement in the warmth of the cabin. Aunt Bertha gave us many old woolen coats.

We usually had some relative staying with us. Mom's brother, Uncle Joe Fulmore, stayed a few summers. Uncle Joe was in his early twenties and had an avid interest in mining for gold. He liked to hunt and enjoyed the rugged outdoor life that our homestead provided. Having another man around was very helpful when Dad had to be away from home, as much of Dad's time was spent buying cattle for a slaughter house located in Eureka. Sometimes Dad would be gone for a month or more. Having Uncle Joe really made my mother feel safer and he could hitch the team to the wagon when it was necessary to

Florence Moon Susan Elizabeth Paddock

go to the Bridgeville store for groceries and the mail. The Bridgeville Post Office and store was about ten miles from our house. My Aunt Florence Paddock spent one winter and summer with us when she was nineteen. Mom really enjoyed having another woman to talk with.

It was fortunate that none of us became extremely ill during our isolation form the rest of the inhabited parts of the world. The winter that Aunt Flo stayed with us we were all sick with the flu. We didn't know where the germ came from as no outsiders had been to visit us for a long time. Mom thought that the germs had been in some of the old clothing that had been given to us. During the winter months, Mom would get out the hand-me-down coats and make them over into clothing for us kids. Perhaps the germs that we caught that winter did come form the old clothes. We were all quite sick but with Mom and Aunt Flo, we managed to survive without the help of a doctor. With the snow piled so high around our place and on the roads we never could have made it to the outside world. When it came to doctoring sick children Dad was as good as a doctor but this particular winter he was gone. He tried to get home but the storm beat him to it. No horse could plow through snow that deep so Dad had to wait for some thaw to take place, which took about six weeks. I can tell you that we were one happy family when he did get home. He always brought Mom and us kids as a treat like candy or oranges.

The red tailed hawks were so thick that our chickens didn't stand a chance unless someone was around to shoot at them. Cele and Sterl would get tin pans and beat on them to scare the hawks away but they couldn't keep this up all day so Mom decided to learn how to shoot the shotgun so she could scare or kill them. One day this huge hawk swooped down and grabbed a hen. She

Ida Belle (Fullmore) Paddock

was squawking and all the other chickens were running around squawking when Mom grabbed the gun and shot the hawk. It killed both the hen and the hawk. We had chicken and dumplings for dinner that night.

Since I was quite young when we moved to Bridgeville, I cannot remember too many things but my sister Lucille has told me many things that I have been recording for some time. I do recall going down to a small stream of water to help Mother do the family washing. Dad had fixed up an outdoor fireplace there for heating water to be used for washing clothes, and during the summer for our baths. Mom would fill the old copper tub about half full, get it good and hot, then add some of her home made soap so that it would melt. After the soap had melted she would add the white clothes and stir them around and around with a broom handle. When she thought that they were clean we would take them out and put them into a bucket of cold water. She kept moving them from one bucket to another until all the soap was washed away. Then she would ring them out by hand. Cele often helped her ring out the sheets. Mom would give Cele one end and she took the other end. Cele held her end very tightly while Mom gently twisted the sheet. The more she twisted the greater the water was rung out. Then Mom would drape the clean clothes over the bushes so they would dry. It was easy to wash clothes during the summer but winter was something left to be desired. Mom had a clothes line strung across the room near the stove for winter drying. Of course we didn't get our clothes as dirty as we did in summer so were able to wear them for a few days before changing. Washing diapers after Cornell's arrival was the biggest washday chore.

This was a very difficult and hard life especially for my Mom as she had 3 children to take care of and had one on the way. After surviving that first long, cold winter on the homestead Cornell was born. He arrived February 10th, just two weeks after Dad had taken us all to Eureka to await his arrival. We were fortunate that most of the early snowfall had melted so we were able to make the trip. On our trips to Eureka we had to ford a small river which wasn't too difficult during the good months of the year. On this trip the river was exceptionally high because of an early thaw. Dad was able to maneuver the team across. Mom was so frightened that she broke down and cried when we reached the other side. The following year Humboldt County built us a bridge over the Van Duzen River so that people living in our area could always get across safely. We stayed with Grandma and Grandpa Paddock during this time. They lived in Eureka on C Street. When Cornell was about three weeks old we returned to our homestead.

Dad didn't always have a hired man, but when he did he usually took him along on cattle buying trips. Dad bought cattle from the Indians. When the Indians were ready to sell they sent word to Dad. Dad and the hired man had to help the Indians round up the cattle as it was open range so the cattle were scattered all over the country. The Indians rode their horses bareback and would ride through the brushy terrain screaming and yelling like mad in order to drive the cattle out. The cattle were easily frightened and would scatter in every direction and they weren't used to people as they had to fend for themselves for their food. They were very much like the wild animals that lived in the area. The Indians never knew just how many head of cattle they owned. They lost quite a few to sickness and cougars. Occasionally a bear would kill a young calf and sometimes a pack of coyotes would make a kill.

The most frightening thing about living on the homestead for us children was the howling of the cougars. One night they came so close to the house that Mom had to bring the dogs inside as she was afraid they would get killed. We always locked the cows and horses in the barn for the night. The cougars always seemed to be on the prowl during the winter months especially when the snow remained on the ground for a long time. Usually a shotgun blast would frighten them away. Mom didn't like shooting the shotgun because the recoil of a 12 gauge would throw her backwards and hurt her shoulder. Mastering the technique for handling any type of gun was very frightening to Mother. She was a city girl and had never been exposed to such primitive living and to top it off she was rather timid in many ways. She relied very heavily on the men that were in her life.

Our cabin was built in a corner of a clearing. The land was quite level surrounding the homestead but there was a small hill that sloped toward the clearing. Cele and Sterl would get into an old wooden barrel and roll down the hill. They did this a great deal of the time to amuse themselves. One day

Sterl coaxed me into the barrel and let it go rolling so fast down the hill with me yelling all the way. It was a bumpy ride too. I was 2 years old the summer that I had the barrel ride. I never got inside that frightening thing again.

Soon after Cornell was born Dad had to go on another buying trip so he had to teach Mom how to milk the cows. She didn't do too well so Dad told her to let Cele help her milk. Cele was six years old and had learned how to milk by helping Dad. The only problem was that her hands weren't strong enough to milk for any length of time. Between Mom and Cele we did have enough milk to drink. What they couldn't get out of the cow the calves got. As time went on Cele became a good milker and she taught Sterling how to milk. Mom was thankful. Dad was too, because all he had to do now was to strip the udder. Stripping the udder was important. It means getting all the milk out. A cow would dry up faster if she wasn't stripped. When the calves were allowed to suck the cows they did the stripping after we had gotten all the milk we needed.

The cows usually freshened in the spring of the year so we had lots of milk. It took 2 to 3 cows to supply us with enough milk to make butter as we had to make some to put away for winter. Our winter supply of butter was made during the fall months so that it would keep better. Cele and Sterl would churn the cream in a small wooden drum that could be turned around and around. If the cream was too cold it would make the butter into small round balls and if it was too warm it would be a big soft mess which was hard to work. Dad built a slanted table top which was held up by four wooden legs. He carved a long paddle out of wood that he attached to the lower end of this table so it could be moved from side to side and up and down. As we poured water over the butter we worked it with the paddle. We had to get all the butter milk out, otherwise the butter would get rancid and would taste terrible. Mother would pack the butter in crocks and make a brine from salt and water. She boiled the salt and water and when it was cool she poured it over the top of the butter. This helped preserve the butter by keeping out the air. A crock lid was put on top to keep out dust or any foreign object. After all this work Mom would put it in the root cellar to keep it as cool as possible. Mom would check it once in awhile to see if it was keeping well.

If it should get a little rancid she would heat the butter and drain off the oil from the melted butter and discard the crud that would settle in the bottom of the pan. The oil could be used for cooking and it wasn't too bad to spread it on bread or pancakes.

Below the house a small stream of water flowed through the trees, down over the mountain to join another small stream. Dad built a cooler on the edge of the stream. Sometimes the butter would be hung in a gunny sack inside the cooler so that the sack just touched the water. This kept other foods cool too. The slats on the cooler were close enough to keep out the small animals such as raccoons, and the openings were large enough to let any breeze that would be prevalent to flow through.

Dad built a smokehouse that cured many slabs of bacon, ham and venison. Drying and smoking meats was the simplest way to keep them from spoiling. Mom canned some venison. She would cut it into cubes and fill the glass jars, put in a mild salt brine and then put them into a large tub, filling it with hot water to cover the tops of the jars, then cook the meat for quite a long time. The brine and cooking helped to preserve the food so that it wouldn't make us sick. Mom used the meat for stews and put some in the stewed beans. Sometimes she would put it into a gravy mixture and serve it on hot biscuits or mashed potatoes.

Wild game was very plentiful so we always had plenty of meat. Dad was an excellent hunter with very keen eyesight in one eye. He was partially blind in the other eye. Dad never killed animals for the sport. He only killed for the food which was a necessity for our survival due to our isolation and economic problems. We usually had our own fowl such as turkeys and chickens but would occasionally run short so Dad would hunt for grouse or quail. I never wanted to eat the quail because I loved to watch them as they ran over the ground with their black topknots nodding back and forth and their song was music to my soul. When I would listen to them it made me feel like they were calling to me. Mom enjoyed a quail dinner very much. When our friends from Eureka came to visit they hunted for quail and would have Mom cook them in her special way. They raved about how delicious the quail were, but I never ate any. Dad would kill a wild hog occasionally and sometimes a wild turkey. The wild hogs were quite dangerous especially if a person was on foot. One charged at my Dad once but he managed to shoot it just before it reached him. It had tusks about three inches long. Some of those wild boars grew quite large, living primarily on acorns. With the advent of man in that remote area they soon became scarce but would on rare occasions become a formidable foe. Dad said that to have one charge out of the brush was like an electric shock to the system. No man went anyplace in the mountains without carrying a high powered rifle. The wild boar meat tasted as good as home grown hogs. Dad butchered the wild hogs just the same as those we raised. He made bacon, hams, and steak from their carcasses. Mom made head cheese from the head and feet. I didn't like it much but everyone else seemed to enjoy it. I hated to see the head cooking in a large pot of water. It made me feel sick to my stomach. After thoroughly cooking the head and feet Mom cooled the meat and then took off the meat and gristle and pressed this by putting it in a pan and then putting a pan on top of it with a heavy sad iron or rack on top of it. Then it was put in the cold cellar to get firm and cold. It was considered a gourmet dish. I forgot to say that she added seasonings and spices to the meat while it was cooking. Mom also tried out the fat and made lard for cooking pastries and other foods. She used some of the tried fat to make soap. The residue or ashes left over from burning the hardwoods made good soap. Mom didn't always have to make soap, only when they were short of money or didn't get to town to buy any. We never had powdered soaps like we use today. To make a liquid soap or shampoo all we had to do was shave or cut the bar soap into small pieces and add water, let soak over night, then heat and stir until entirely melted. To make it smell good Mom would add a little cologne or perfume.

Dad always planted a garden so we had fresh vegetables during the summer months. We had some rhubarb plants which Mom used to make sauce and her delicious rhubarb pies. Mom made the pie crust with lard as we didn't have the vegetable oil shortening then. Lard really made delicious pastries. Our small strawberry patch furnished us with fresh fruit and preserves. We always looked forward to the season that brought us the luscious berries as Mom made delicious strawberry shortcake. She made the hot biscuit kind which was my favorite.

Lucille Rebecca Paddock

Cottontail rabbits would invade the garden at times. They usually ended up on our dinner table. If I'd known they were rabbits I don't think I would have eaten them.

Sometimes Cele, Sterl, and I looked like three little urchins left over from the slums area in New York. We wore baggy garments with patches in many places. It really didn't matter how we looked just as long as we were clean and well fed because we didn't have many visitors due to our isolation. Mom always had a couple of good outfits for us to wear when someone came or we went to town.

On top of the mountain over the hill from our house, there was a beautiful, crystal clear blue lake. Many people said that it was bottomless. The plants grew lush and green around the lake. We picked the tender watercress shoots to put in our salads or ate them as we picked them. I really enjoyed the peppery taste. Other times we would pick mustard greens for Mom to cook. I always ate many of the young budded plants as I was picking. Dad liked dandelion greens so we helped him pick tender shoots from the center of the plant. Money was scarce and we were really quite poor so had to supplement our diet with some of natures foods. Our domesticated ducks and geese spent a lot of time on the lake. They nested in thick plants near the edge of the lake. Cele would gather the eggs for Mom which she used in cooking many delicious dishes. We also liked the eggs scrambled for breakfast. They tasted just like chicken eggs and the only difference was that they were larger and went further. We didn't have good luck raising ducks and geese. There were too many predators.

Once Sterling got lost and it took almost the entire day to find him. He was four years old at this time and felt that he was as grown up as any man on the place so decided to go down to the area that the men had been clearing. It was quite a long walk and a very warm summer day so Sterl decided to take a rest when he got tired. Dad had left an old scrub out there and it had been pulled up over some small tree stumps and limbs so Sterl decided to get under it so that he would be out of the sun and it also gave him some protection just in case a wild animal should venture near. He fell asleep and stayed there until almost dark. All the men were going through the bushes and trees yelling as loud as they could but Sterl didn't hear them. The hired man had covered that area and since it was in an open area he didn't think Sterl was anywhere near as he returned home to tell the others that there was no sight of him anywhere near the clearing. As the sun began to set the air took on a chill which woke Sterl from his long afternoon sleep. Dad had taken the dog and gone in the opposite direction so the dog wasn't any help. Dad and the others conferred for awhile and decided that it might be better if they stayed closed together while searching. The center person would yell and then all the others would yell at once, thus creating more noise. Then all of them would stop and listen. They had just begun this procedure when Sterl came running toward them. He wanted to know what the yelling was all about.

OUR LIFE ON THE TRINITY RIVER

Our good friend Dr. Eugene Fountain owned a ranch on the Trinity River. He needed someone to operate the ranch so he asked Dad if he would like the job. Mother was delighted with the prospect of living close to neighbors and a small town that consisted of a general store, post office, and hotel with an eating place. Dad knew that it was necessary to move away from the Bridgeville homestead because Lucille had reached the age where her schooling had to be considered. It wasn't hard to sell the homestead. All the land around it was owned by a large cattle operation and they were very happy to buy us out. The day that we left our homestead was a beautiful spring morning with delicate green buds popping out of the scrub oak trees and dogwood trees. The whole mountain seemed to have taken on a delicate green color which created an expectancy within our hearts. We were going to a new and exciting life. Anticipation reigned with all of us. A better life for all of us was just over the hills and valleys, down the mountain and across the rivers once again. Even the horses seemed excited and did a lot of snorting as we climbed up to our seats on the wagon. We journeyed to Eureka and stayed there for a couple of months before moving to the Fountain ranch. This gave Mom a chance to get caught up on her social life and to do some shopping. We stayed in Grandma and Grandpa's house on C Street. This gave us children a chance to get reacquainted with our relatives that we hadn't seen for a long time.

One thing that I enjoyed doing while in Eureka was to walk down the board sidewalks, ride on the trolley cars, and watch the women as they walked down the street, swishing their long dresses and flipping their heads to show off the feathers and ribbons that adorned their colorful hats. One day when I was walking down town with Mother I watched a man and boy that was ahead of us. The man walked over to the side of the street and spit out a lot of yellow juice. As he started off, his son copied his Dad by spitting too. The boy was about six years old. This fascinated me so much that I kept pestering Mom to tell me about the yellow juice. Mom thought that it was a nasty dirty habit that she couldn't stand, and to chew tobacco was the very worst habit any one could have. One day when I was with Dad I saw a man spit into a spittoon. We were in the lobby of a hotel and I was sitting on a leather sofa and the man was sitting on the other end near a shiny brass spittoon. He spit several times as I sat there. I just couldn't take my eyes off of him. I think this bothered him as he left after a little while. Dad had gone up to a man's room to talk to him about buying a team of horses and Dad thought it best for me to wait in the lobby. I was about four years old and when told to do something we did just as we were told so I didn't budge from that sofa. I think that being somewhat scared helped to keep me in one place.

During our stay in Eureka we were introduced to the automobile. Mom's sister, Aunt Bertha and her husband, Uncle Fred, had a Ford car so they took us for several rides around the town. Only a few people had automobiles. Most of the people were still traveling by horse and buggy or wagon.

There were many teams of large horses such as the Percherons which were very good draft horses. My cousin, Will Poyfaire, had a team of Clydesdales. They were huge and strong enough to pull a heavy load of merchandise. Cousin Will took Sterl and I for a ride around town. We were perched way up high on the seat of the wagon and I was sitting between Will and Sterl so I wouldn't fall. Will's language was something to be desired. He did a lot of strong loud cussing as he maneuvered the team through and around traffic.

Our short stay in Eureka introduced us to a number of new things. We didn't have to go outside to the outhouse when nature called. The flush toilet was a thing of mystery to me. I wanted to keep pulling the chain to see the water come out. The wooden tub was made from oak staves with a band of steel around the top on the outside. The wooden tub had belonged to Grandma which she gave us when we moved to the homestead.

I was four when we moved to the Fountain Ranch located high above the Trinity River. Mom and Dad loaded the wagon the day before our departure from Eureka. Mom and Dad sat on the seat of the wagon and she held Cornell on her lap. Cele, Sterl, and I rode in the back just behind the front seat. Dad made it very comfortable for us with quilts and pillows. Cele kept Sterl and me entertained for most of the trip. Sterl and I slept for awhile so that gave Cele a rest.

The Fountain Ranch was across the river from the town and school house. A swinging bridge was our direct connection with the town. To get to the ranch we had to cross the bridge, and to get to the town we had to cross the bridge. The men would get off their horses and lead them across the bridge. Many horses would balk and refuse to get on the bridge. The bridge was about three feet wide with large steel cables along each side. (Cele said "Maybe less than 3 ft"). It would sway or swing something fierce when anyone went over it. It was much better if only one person went over the bridge at a time. The first time I had to go over the bridge was a frightening experience for me. Dad carried me. Cele walked over it very self assured and Sterling ran all the way over which he did every time he crossed the bridge. Mom got down on her hands and knees and crawled all the way. She was so frightened, and thereafter the only time she would go over the bridge was because of an emergency or absolute necessity.

The ranch house was luxury for all of us. It was a cottage type building, painted white, with a covered porch along one side and end. Vines like ivy and hops trailed up the posts and some were twined around wires that were strung from the floor to the roof line. Many of us slept out there during the hot summer months. A cool breeze would drift up the river and help cool the night air. After living in a two room cabin this home was like a palace to us. Mom enjoyed the large kitchen with many cupboards and enough space for a good sized breakfast table. There was a large dining room with a long table that seated twelve people. Mom always kept a white linen table cloth ironed to perfection on it all the time, even if the tired dusty hired hands ate there. During the hot summer months the workers washed up outside where a basin, soap, and roller towels were provided. These were placed on a wooden bench that held several basins. The basins were blue and white enamel on the outside and white inside.

All of the basins had chips of enamel off the outside and around the rim which showed that they had been used very much. The men would fill the basin full of cool water from the faucet near the corner of the bench. Then they would wet their faces and arms, apply a thick lather of soap and scrub with their hands until all the grime was gone. Some the them washed their hair and combed it down so that it looked like a skull cap. A old square mirror hung on the wall above the basin which had a few blank spots because the silver had been rubbed off the back of the glass. A tin cup hung from a hook above the faucet. Sometimes the men would drink and let the water run down their chins onto their shirt fronts. This helped to cool them off and the water would dry fast.

The house was partly surrounded by cherry trees. Walking beneath them seemed like a huge forest to me. The trees had never been pruned so their branches hung low to the ground. Once I ate so many cherries, pits, and all, that I became quite ill. Robert Fountain fell out of the top of a large cherry tree. It happened that first summer that we were there. Uncle Joe Fulmore and Harry Stocks rushed him to a hospital which was about eighty miles away. Robert did not survive as his stomach was ruptured in the fall. All of us children were very sad. We loved to play with Robert and he was such a kind boy. He was several years older than we were so we looked up to him for entertainment and fun.

The pastures surrounding the house had huge clumps of wild roses which would bloom all summer. Sometimes they were a solid red color that really brightened up the countryside. They were very thorny plants that really hurt when you pierced yourself. I often played around them so got pricked quite often. Mom didn't want me playing in the wild roses but I loved to go there and would sneak away whenever I could. In the fall of the year, the bushes would be covered with rose hips or seed pods. I would pick them and Cele would help me string them so that I could use them for a string of beads. I only picked the bright red ones. The wild birds and animals liked to use a clump of wild roses for their home. They provided a wonderful nesting place for the blue birds. Chipmunks liked to scurry around underneath the dense, tangled mass of rose vines. Once a big blow snake came out from beneath a clump and scared me very much. They made a funny blow sound like escaping air from a person's mouth. Their color was very similar to the tan color of the soil and were hard to see sometimes.

The Fountain ranch was across the river from all outside activities but even with that scary swinging bridge we did attend most of the school functions. Sterl and Cele had to cross it every day to get to school. It didn't bother them in the least but Mom and I were always timid about crossing it. The Trinity river was deep and quite swift but not very wide where we lived. Cattle and wagons could ford it about a mile up river. Once Dad was taking a herd of cattle across and his horse got too far down stream and slipped into some very deep water. The horse panicked and floundered around so that Dad fell off. During the threshing around the horse stepped on Dad's back and pushed him down to the bottom of the river. The shoe of the horse cut a shoe shape of cloth out of Dad's flannel shirt and left a deep imprint on his back. Dad almost drowned. It was a dangerous river because of the tall steep banks as well as its depth and swiftness. Its cascading waters went tumbling through the deep canyon very vigorously. It was about a five hundred foot drop to the river from where our house was situated. The drop was almost straight down. Quite a few scrub manzanita bushes grew on its banks as well as other small plants. Sometimes cattle would plunge to their death if they lost their footing while trying to reach for a mouth watering morsel of low growing plants.

Once when a rider and his horse were crossing the swinging bridge an eagle flew toward them and the horse became panic stricken. He jumped up and down. Lost his footing and fell four hundred or more feet to his death. The rider clung to the cables and thus managed to save himself from plunging to the river below. He hung onto the cables so hard that his hands were quite raw from the twisting of the cables as they swung back and forth. After the bridge stopped its violent swaying he crossed over to our place. He swore that he would never take a horse over any swinging bridge again. Dad always had medication for such injuries so he treated and bandaged the man's hands. I don't remember who the man was.

In our back yard there were a couple of rope swings hanging from some tall oak trees. The ropes for the swings seemed to me to be at least twenty feet long. The seat was a wooden board with grooves at each end which fitted into the rope and held the board in place. Cele and Sterl used to swing so far out they could glimpse the Trinity river far below. If they didn't hold on tight to the ropes they could be thrown over the bank and go tumbling down to the river below. Mom worried a lot but she couldn't keep an eye on them all the time. Cele and Sterl got me into the swing once and pushed me way out, far enough to see the river and it frightened me so much that I started to cry and begged them to stop the swing. They laughed at me and Sterl laughed so hard that he bent over and rolled around a few times. Mom heard me screaming and came on the run to see what was the matter with me. She stopped the swing and gave Cele and Sterl a good tongue lashing. After that the only time that I could swing was when Mom or Dad helped me.

It's a miracle that one of us kids didn't get killed while living on the Fountain Ranch. There was a fence strung all along the top of the cliffs and around some of the pastures where our animals grazed. It was made of sheep wire with a couple of stands of barbed wire at the top. Cele and Sterling used to walk along the cliffs, outside of the fence on their way to and from school. Cele wasn't too keen on it but Sterl was sort of a dare-devil so he always managed to get Cele to go along with some of his ideas. They would hang onto the fence as they inched their way along the bank. One slip and they could have rolled and plunged to their death. Dad didn't know that they were doing this for a long time. When he found out about it he put a stop to their shenanigans. This was a shortcut for them on their way home from school and they couldn't go through the pastures because of the bulls and stallions. A couple of the bulls were very dangerous and one stallion was a killer.

Dad had bought the killer stallion from a neighbor and he wanted to use it for breeding purposes. The reason that the neighbor sold it to Dad was because it had trampled a man to death. The neighbor was going to kill the stallion and when Dad found out about it he asked the neighbor if he would be willing to sell him to Dad. The stallion was kept in a corral that was made out of logs about ten inches thick and it was about eight feet high. A stall with a roof over it was at one side of the hay barn. A watering trough was in one corner of the corral. No one had to enter the corral to take care of the horse. Hay was pitched down into the manger form the hay loft. The stallion was always trying to get out of his prison. Sometimes he would rear up on his hind legs and stomp the rails, whinnying and snorting like a wild beast. Sometimes I thought that he might breathe out fire, especially when his eyes would get such a mean and wild look. Cele, Sterl and I would climb up the rails to the top of the fence and watch him. The stallion scared us off that fence lots of times. Soon after Dad brought the horse home I climbed over the rail fence and was inside with the stallion. I was only about a couple of feet away from the fence when the stallion charged out of the shed snorting and pawing the ground. I turned and started climbing that fence so fast, and just as I reached the top rail he was breathing on me. I screamed and Dad came running and helped me down. I will never forget that horses wild eyes, his large white teeth ready to grab me. He opened his mouth and bared his teeth like a savage wolf might when confronted with danger. Whenever anything had to be done for the stallion the men always took pitch forks with them and no one ever went inside the corral alone. When they did go in they stayed near the fence or near the door or manger. Once Dad was repairing the manger and the stallion almost got him. The hired man was trying to keep the horse away by yelling and swishing the pitchfork in front of his face. The hired man was protected as he stood behind some posts but Dad was exposed. The horse was so quick like a flash he darted inside the shelter and reared up ready to strike with his front feet. Dad just rolled inside the manger in time and was able to crawl out through an opening in the planks. Soon after this narrow escape Dad decided that it was too dangerous to keep such a mean animal so he had him shot and buried. They shot him in the corral and then put his body on a scrub and hauled it away down to the far pasture where it was buried. I guess that stallion had served his purpose. Not long after his death we had a beautiful little sorrel filly which Dad gave to us kids for our very own. We named her Dolly and we loved her and she loved us.

Just below the house was our covered spring-house where Mom kept our fresh foods such as milk and vegetables. Mom always had a crock full of mincemeat and one of sauerkraut plus smaller crocks of butter. We didn't have any type of refrigeration in those days but could use hunks or blocks of ice if we could get them. Occasionally we were able to get a block of ice, and when we did we always had ice cream. Dad usually made the mixture and supervised the freezing process. Cele and Sterl would help by turning the crank on the freezer. Dad would take over the last part of the freezing as by this time Cele and Sterl were getting tired and as the mixture got harder it required a stronger hand. It was the most delicious ice cream that I have ever eaten. Dad would take the paddles out and give each of us a sample or let us lick the paddles. Then he would cover the container and pack it with rock salt and ice and let it ripen or become more firm. The spring-house kept things really cool as the water that trickled out of the side of the bluff came from deep down and was always cold.

None of us children were allowed to go down to the spring-house because it was too dangerous. A narrow path curved around the side of the bluff to the cooler and just one slip could send a body plunging down to the river below. Usually the men would go down to store the food or bring it back when Mom needed it for a meal. Occasionally Mom would go down but she didn't relish the chore as she was frightened of heights. One day I decided that I would go down the path to the spring-house. I made it down and enjoyed sitting for awhile beside the cool little stream of water. It was just a trickle but sufficient to create a delightful place for a child to enjoy. I sampled some of the food from the crocks and sipped the cool water. Bright green plants grew on the ground around and inside the spring house. It seemed like I was in a different world and I stayed for a long time. I was in another world until I heard Mom and Uncle Joe calling my name. I started up the path in a hurry and when I came to the steep part I slipped and fell and rolled over the bank. I started to slide down the steep bank. In my fright I grabbed for some small growing shrubs that were fortunately quite thick in this spot. I hung on as tight as I could and yelled for Mom. Uncle Joe heard me and was there in a flash. He told me to hang on and not move until he got back. He dashed up to the barn and got a long rope which he tied around a tree and then around his waist. It would have been impossible for him to rescue me without this precaution.

He very slowly worked his way down beside me and carefully gathered me up in his arms. I put my arms around his neck and held on while he dug his feet into the rather loose covering of soil and used his hands on the rope to help propel us out of this predicament. I probably wouldn't be alive today if it hadn't been for Uncle Joe. Dad was gone on a cattle buying trip. I don't think Mom could have ever gotten me back up the steep bank. Well, that scared me so much that I never went down to the spring-house again. Cele and Sterl were cautioned against going too.

We had one critter that was a holy pest as far as Cornell and I were concerned. It was a bummer lamb that Sterl and Cele raised by the bottle method. They named him Eekie and he followed them wherever they went on the ranch. For some reason when Eekie was about half grown he started bunting Cornell and me down every time he saw us. He really kept watch over us until someone came to rescue us. One hot summer day Cornell and I were walking down the dusty road which ran in front of our house. Eekie spied us and came running and gave each of us a hard butt, down we went falling in about an inch of dust. Our faces were covered with a heavy layer of dust as well as our clothes. As we rolled over our hair took up much of the powdery stuff. We were a sight to behold. Cornell was crying and screaming very loud while I tried to get up so I could push Eekie away from us. He butted me down each time I tried to get up. We were at his mercy. When this happened Eekie had grown to a full sized ram. Cornell's tears mixed with the dust which made mud streaks on his face. After Eekie laid me flat several times, I started screaming and crying. It was some time before Mom missed us. She sent Cele out looking for us. Cele helped us get up and brushed some of the dust out of our clothes and took us back to the house. Mom was quite angry as she had to give us both a bath and put a

William Cornell "Nelly" Paddock

clean outfit of clothes on us again. In fact she was so angry by the time she had us cleaned up that she told Dad he would have to get rid of the sheep. Mom just couldn't stand to see Cornell's beautiful blond hair all covered with dirt. She kept his hair in a Dutch bob and even put bluing in the rinse water to keep it looking like a platinum blonde. She followed this procedure until Cornell was about four years old.

A favorite haunt of Sterling's was a small pond about a half mile form our house. He loved to collect big bull frogs and bring them home. I guess they were really toads but they were very large. He often came home muddy and wet up to his waist. No matter how much he got scolded for doing this, he always went back. We would play with the toads and put them beneath an old galvanized tub at night. Sterl would put a couple of large rocks on top of the tub so that it wouldn't get tipped over. Do you know, those frogs were never there the next morning. Sterl thought someone had let them out. We did every thing that we could think of to keep those frogs from getting out. No one could tell us why they were gone in the morning. Years later I found out that the toads just dug down into the earth and buried themselves. One day I went down to the pond with Sterl. He used a stick and prodded into the mud and water which disturbed the toads so that they would jump and then Sterl would jump after them. If he fell down that was fine with him just as long as he captured his prey. I tried to catch one and to my dismay I fell flat on my face in the muddy water. I got up sputtering and wiping the mud and water away from my face with my hands and getting out of there as fast as I could. I wanted to go home because I was all wet but Sterl coaxed me to stay so that my clothes would get dry before Mom saw me. I was quite miserable but I stayed and did enjoy watching Sterl splash around and catch toads. Some times he stuffed them in his pockets and after he had caught a couple he would put them in a bag that had a draw string so they couldn't escape. It seemed like Sterl was always in trouble and I was close behind.

As I said before, Sterl was a little dare devil and didn't seem to fear anything. For a kid that only weighed a little over two pounds at birth, he was an average sized boy for his age and very wiry. When he was six years old he would get out in the middle of the swinging bridge, grab hold of one cable and swing back and forth, and every time he crossed the bridge he would run fast and try to make it sway as much as possible. Cele always tried to stop him but didn't have any success.

Cornell and I were too young to attend school while we lived at Willow Creek. Cele and Sterl attended school. Cele was in the first grade and Sterl was in kindergarten class. It was a one room school. Their teacher was married to an Indian that was a half breed. Cele and Sterl were the only white children in the school. All the others were Indian or half breeds. Cele and Sterl caught head lice from the Indian children. Mom used coal oil on their heads which killed the lice. Cele had long blonde hair in two braids and needed two coal oil treatments. Sterl's hair was cut quite short so required only one treatment. Mom wrapped a cloth around their heads after putting on the oil and left it on for quite a few hours. Dad reported it to a county nurse so she checked all the children and teachers in the school and treated them all for head lice. She also checked them for tuberculosis and found several children with the disease. Mom was forever scrubbing us from head to toe and she boiled our clothes in an old copper tub after this. Cele's and Sterl's clothes received extra special cleaning. I think that it was good that Mom and Dad were so concerned as many people, especially the Indians, were very susceptible to tuberculosis. Many people died from this disease.

While living at Willow Creek we lived under the shadow of prisoners that were camped across the river from our home. They were chain gangs and were carving roads out of the mountain sides. Once I saw some of the prisoners and they had chains around their ankles and were dressed in drab gray striped coveralls and all of them wore visor like caps. The work that they did was very hard and difficult as they had to carry thousands of rocks to build up the sides of the roads so that they would not wash out during the heavy rains that Humboldt County is noted for. The law had tents set up for sleeping and cooking and office space. The shackles were never removed from the feet of the prisoners. I heard Dad talking about the sores on the feet and ankles of the men. When the sores got too bad the irons were removed and medication was applied to the wounds. The shackles were then attached to the wrists and they were chained to a heavy piece of metal. These men were considered very dangerous because they had committed a murder or several murders. It was a very miserable life for any human being especially during the cold winter months when the snow and cold rains arrived. The prisoners were taken back to Eureka and put in jail when the weather became too bad for working. The prisoners came from jails situated all over the state. They were always trying to escape and a couple managed to do just that. The guards alerted all of the people to be on the look out for them and to be extremely careful if the citizens of Willow Creek should encounter them. This was a very rugged, mountainous area with deep forests that made searching very difficult. They found the escaped prisoners about a week later near Eureka.

Dad supplied the prison camp with fresh meat, bacon, hams and fresh pork, also beef. During the summer we furnished them with vegetables from our garden. They also bought milk and eggs from us. One summer Mom and Dad made gallons of catsup which they sold. They simmered the tomato juice and spices for hours so that it would get thick. They did this outside since the days were very warm. A large sheet of steel was used to put over the outdoor fireplace and it would get red hot sometimes. Too hot for most cooking so Mom would have to let it cool some before putting kettles of food on the top. The hired men usually fired it up so stoked it full of hardwood not realizing that it would burn too hot. The catsup was cooked in large galvanized tubs. When it was thick enough Mom and Dad would bottle it. Dad had set up an old wood burning stove outside that Mom could also cook on during the summer months. Mom usually had a crowd to cook for, hired men, the family, and relatives of Dr. Fountain. Sometimes Aunt Bertha and Uncle Fred Moore would bring their four boys and stay for several days. The extra stove saw much use during our stay in Willow Creek.

When we had a large crowd for dinner or lunch Dad usually helped Mother cook and serve the meal. Cele helped by setting the table and carrying food to the guests. I coaxed Mom to let me help too. Once I had a large bowl of macaroni to carry and I dropped it. Mom's clean floor wasn't clean any longer. Guess it was just too much to expect from a four year old. I was humiliated and hurt when Mom scolded me in front of all those people. I guess I wanted to show off since I had a pretty new white dress and had a ribbon tied in the top of my hair. I was always fishing for compliments whenever I got dressed up which wasn't very often. I would ask various people if I looked "tweet" today. Tweet meant sweet.

Since we sold quite a lot of pork to the prison camp, Dad set aside an entire day for butchering usually 3 or 4 hogs. Much of the pork was cured which took a good deal of time, especially the curing of the hams. It took a long time for the water to reach the boiling stage. This was the first thing to be done for the killing of the pigs. I didn't like this part because sometimes I could hear them squeal and I thought that they were hurting them. They sure did a lot of squealing while being caught. They were put in the huge trough and covered with the boiling water after they were bled and then gutted out. This would loosen the stiff hairs on their hide so that they could be scraped off. After scraping them thoroughly the men would scrub them with a stiff brush to get the skin good and clean. Then they were cut up and the parts to be smoked were seasoned and hung in the smoke house. Dad sure could make good bacon and hams. Also some very good sausage. Mom made head cheese from the parts of the head. Nothing was wasted.

I will never forget Uncle Marion Paddock dunking Cornell in the barrel of rain water that sat beneath the eaves of the house. Mom and Dad had gone to Eureka for a few days and left Uncle Marion to baby sit us. Cornell was about three years old and was still wetting his bed every night. Uncle Marion got fed up with the business of changing his bed every day and airing it out. Sometimes he wet his pants which aggravated the problem considerably. This was just too much for Uncle Mary (as we called him). He blew his top. When he got angry everyone had better watch out. Guess it was his curly red hair that set him on fire, at least that is what we thought. It didn't take us long to scatter when his angry voice started booming. Well, he just lifted Cornell up by the seat of his pants, flipped him upside down and dunked him head first into the barrel of water. He kept doing this many times, in and out. The rest of us kids thought that he was drowning Cornell so we all started to cry and scream at him. He was mad enough to drown Cornell and might have if we hadn't made such a screaming ruckus. Poor Cornell, it took him quite awhile to get over his water bath and I don't think he ever got over his fear of Uncle Mary. Mom and Dad were both very angry with my Uncle and never trusted him to look after us again. Cornell shied away from that rain barrel. Mom kept it there to catch the rain water so she could wash our woolen clothes and hair in the soft water. Our hair felt like silk and shone like a golden coin after having been shampooed with rain water.

Cornell and I had a buggy experience soon after we moved to Willow Creek. There was an old dilapidated shed that had been used for a woodshed and was located quite a distance from the house. Cornell and I were doing a little exploring and went inside the shed to see if we could find some interesting things. We played around digging in the wood chips. I wasn't too interested but Cornell didn't want to go and play outside so he stayed inside. I felt something biting me and was excited when I saw lots of little red brown bugs jumping on my clothes and many were on my legs and feet. All of sudden Cornell tore out of the shed yelling that something was chewing on him. He was literally covered with the bugs. He had made the mistake of sitting down while playing inside. Guess he thought he was looking for treasures. He had hundreds of fleas on him. He jumped up and down and started crying and running toward the house. Mom heard the commotion that we were making so came outside to see what was causing us to make so much noise. She threw her hands up in the air and said "Don't come near me" and "Stay outside while I fill the bathtub with water". We started to take off our clothes and Cornell kept hopping around while we waited for Mom to come back. Mom came out soon with a sheet that she wrapped around Cornell and then carried him into the house and put him in the tub of warm water. She made me stay outside while she took care of Cornell. She put so much soap on his head that it ran down into his eyes and then the screaming started. Dad was working near the corral so he came running to find out if his help was needed. They got Cornell out of the tub and flushed the fleas down the drain with some very hot water. By the time they got the tub ready for me I had lots of flea bites all over me. The water felt so good as it washed the fleas away. Dad put some medication on our bites so that they didn't itch so much. Those fleas seemed to be starved. Dad and the hired man burned down the shed which killed the fleas. Dad spread some kind of powdery material all around the house to keep the fleas from invading our home.

One Easter I got a pet rabbit so Dad built a cage for it and nailed the cage to a tree trunk just high enough for me to reach when I stood on a wooded stool. I didn't know much about taking care of animals as I was only four years old. Dad taught me how to feed and water the bunny rabbit. I fed my pet grass that I cut from around the trees and some alfalfa hay. Besides feeding and watering him each day I did a lot of talking to him. I like the way he wiggled or twitched his little nose. His brown fur was so soft and I thought he was the best pet in the world. One morning when I went out to feed him I found him dead. I thought that I had done something to kill him. Dad explained that he was a little wild rabbit and that sometimes they get sick. He told me that I had taken real good care of the little baby rabbit and loved him which was the important thing.

One summer Dad rased a beard which was red and quite bushy. Mom didn't cater to his beard. She kept after him to cut it so when Aunt Florence came up to visit with us, Mom got her to help in getting rid of Dad's beard. Dad was a very sound sleeper so one night after he went to bed and was sleeping soundly Mom and Aunt Florence snipped all the whiskers off one side of his face. When Dad woke up the next morning he was shocked to find out that half of his beard was missing. When he looked in the mirror he started to laugh. Mom and Aunt Flo joined in and were glad that Dad had a good sense of humor. All of us kids came running to see what was so funny. Dad looked really funny so we joined in the laughter too.

Dr. Eugene Fountain and wife Susie always spent a couple of weeks with us each summer. He was a dentist like his father, Dr. Matthew Fountain. It was always lots of fun when friends and relatives came to visit us. Their visits meant picnics, dances, and just visiting sessions where lots of interesting things were told. They always brought a good supply of groceries, many things that we didn't get very often, and they always included a bag of candies for us children.

All the people around our part of the country would gather occasionally for a dance and midnight supper. Several violin players would provide the music. I always enjoyed listening to the haunting strains of the fiddles. All of the children would sit around the dance floor next to the wall and watch the dancers. When we got so sleepy that we just couldn't stay awake we would crawl under a table or behind the stove and sleep. All the noise in the world wouldn't wake us up. Some of the older children would sneak into the pantry where all the food was stored and snitch a piece of cake or sandwich. There was always so much food that a few pieces wouldn't be missed. Many of the women tried to out do each other in their baking so we had the very best pies and cakes of almost every kind imaginable. Some of the women would feed all of the younger children long before the dance would end so that they could go to sleep.

Many of the parties became quite wild and noisy as the evening progressed. Quite a few of the men were single so they did a lot of flirting with the women, married and single alike. The school house was the only place large enough to hold a party. It had a large room where the pupils sat at their desks and another small room that we called an ante room which was a place for coats and storage of materials such as books and paper. The women would set up a table in the ante room for the foods that they brought. They would drape a large table cloth over the table and it usually hung to the floor to hide the extra boxes of goodies. One night while the party was going on I hid under the table and as I remember Sterl and another boy were there too. They were looking for goodies to snitch. One of the men had quite a thing going for my mother so one night I was hiding beneath that table and Mom came in to start preparations for the midnight feast and then a tall man came in and pinched Mom on her bottom and tried to kiss her. She left in a hurry. The men in those days did a lot of pinching the women on their derriere. Most of the single men were miners or ranch hands and usually showed up at a festive gathering in the little school house.

Mother was a small woman (only five feet and one inch) and she weighed about one hundred and ten pounds. She was afraid of many things, especially the lightening and thunder. Dad was just the opposite. He enjoyed the rumble of the electric storm. He taught us to also enjoy the excitement of a storm. We would sit on the front porch and watch the streaks of lightening come to the earth sometimes hitting trees and splitting them in half. The lightening would spiral down a huge fir tree until it grounded itself. Our house was equipped with lightening rods so we were not too concerned. I have never seen such spectacular electric storms since we moved form Willow Creek. They were the grand daddies of all storms. Such storms are still invigorating to me.

OUR DAYS AND YEARS ON KNEELAND PRAIRIE

When I was about five years old we moved from Dr. Fountain's Willow Creek ranch. Our stay there was for only about two years. Dad and Mom were able to save enough money to buy a 340 acre ranch on Kneeland Prairie in Humboldt Co. for three thousand dollars. The year was 1917.

We did not have an automobile so we moved to Eureka by horses and wagon. I only remember one trip to Eureka and that was the trip that took us to our new home. Dad covered the hay wagon with a canvas to protect us and the household goods from rain and dust. Our move was in the fall of the year so the roads were plenty dusty and we were prepared for rain too, which came in very quickly but not lasting too long. The rain would settle the dust but it also puddled in low lying areas of the road making mud. The road was a winding two rut, narrow and sometimes very steep road to travel. In a couple of places Dad had to tie a fir tree to the back of the wagon to help hold the wagon from going too fast and to save the brakes. If the wagon went too fast it would run into the horses and cause a serious accident.

We stayed with friends the first night out. The next morning we left in another rain storm. This slowed us down considerably because it was harder for the two horses to pull the heavy wagon thru a gooey mess of muck. Late that night we arrived at Grandmother's and Grandfather's house in Eureka.

We were very happy to be at Grandma's house and to be given a good hot dinner. All of us children were very tired and sleepy so Grandma got out her home made quilts and we rolled up in them on the parlor floor and were soon asleep, contented and so happy.

We stayed at Grandma and Grandpa Paddock's home on C Street for a few weeks before moving to Kneeland. While there Sterl had an accident splitting kindling to help Grandpa out. He was only six years old, quite small to use a hatchet. He split his thumb in half. When I saw the blood I started screaming and ran into the house which alerted Mom to something going on outside. She ran out and took Sterl's split finger in her hand and held the parts together. She yelled to Cele to bring out a cloth to wrap around Sterl's finger. Cele grabbed one of Dad's clean handkerchiefs and dashed outside. Mom wound the handkerchief around Sterl's thumb and then she held his hand up while they dashed up the street to the hospital. It was a Catholic hospital and was about six blocks away. The doctor sewed the two parts of the finger together and bandaged it. The doctor didn't know if it would heal since the two parts were almost totally severed. It healed and never gave Sterl any trouble except for the fingernail which grew rather thick and heavy down the middle of the finger.

One day Grandma asked Dad to go to the store to get some milk so I asked Dad to let me hold the money. He gave me the fifty cent piece and told me to hold it tight in my hand, but I didn't hold it tight enough. It slipped out of my grasp and rolled along the wooden sidewalk and fell into a crack. I thought it was lost forever but Dad said he could get it out but would have to go back home to get a crowbar so he could pry the plank up. I had to wait right where the money fell down the crack until Dad got back. An old man came along and wanted to know what I was doing. When I told him he got down on his knees and looked to see if I had told him the truth. He said that I should have a big chew of gum on the end of a stick and then I could get the money out. Of course none of us had a big chaw of gum which seemed like a silly idea to me. I was only four years old then and now that I am old, I realize that the old man's idea wasn't too far fetched. Dad got the money out and re-nailed the plank and we proceeded down the street to the store. Fifty cents in those days was a lot of money. Many people only earned a dollar a day for their labors. This taught me a good lesson in being very careful with money.

I was only two years old when World War I broke out. It ended in 1918. Our country entered the war when our allies cried for help. While at Grandmother's home, Aunt Cele was attending a school in Eureka and she was eight years old. The Red Cross recruited every segment of the population to assist them in such things as rolling bandages which Cele's third grade class did to help the cause. Each girl was given a white uniform with the red cross on the sleeve and each wore a Red Cross cap. Only the girls participated in this project. I wanted to be a helper in the worst way so hung around while the girls were working. I was only three and a half years old so presented a nuisance at times. One of the Red Cross leaders was sympathetic to my eagerness to participate so she gave me a toy nursing set that was similar to the Red Cross packets. I was a very happy little girl and even learned how to roll bandages before the project ended. Aunt Cele also paraded with her class through the streets of Eureka to drum up money for war bonds.

While at Willow Creek I developed a case of rickets and the glands in my neck were swollen in quite large lumps. This of course was caused from my poor appetite. One food I couldn't stand was warm milk so I refused to drink it. Dad would buy ice when we were in Eureka when he could get it so that he could entice me into drinking milk. When he couldn't get ice he would put my glass of milk on the window sill at night and open the window some so that the cool night air would get the milk cold. With some cajoling from Dad I would drink the milk. The doctor also prescribed iodine for painting my neck to help reduce the swollen glands. This all seemed to help but I still remained a skinny little girl.

Our stay at Grandma's wasn't very long as Dad had the house on Kneeland ready for our occupancy. Dad loaded all of our personal belongings into the wagon the night before we were to take off on our journey up the mountain to our new home. Towering redwood trees lined the winding and sometimes steep dirt road and wild rhododendrons were blooming beneath the great giants. Lots of ferns and many other types of plant life were abundant on the carpet of needles beneath the trees. Around noon time we came out of the forest and we welcomed the warmth of the sunshine and open spaces. Mom and Grandma had put up a picnic lunch for us so Dad stopped the team and unhitched them so they could have a rest and a chance to eat some of the tall prairie grasses that were still lush and green. One type of grass that grew all over the prairie really fascinated me. It was called "wild oats" and the tips of the stems had little seeds that looked like rattle snake rattles that would quiver in the breeze. It was a very good food source for the cattle as well as the heavy deer population. Of course the wild turkeys and birds like to eat the seeds too. This was the food that our tame turkeys ate during the summer when I herded them over the hills. They also consumed lots of grasshoppers.

Our ranch was on the top of Kneeland Prairie. A man by the name of Kneeland homesteaded the land. If I remember right our ranch was three hundred and forty acres. It had some good timber on it and Freshwater Creek wound its way from the top of the Red Knoll to eventually end up in Humboldt Bay and then out into the Pacific Ocean. Most of the land was for grazing livestock but we did have a few fields that could be cultivated and planted into oats or barley which we used for hay. We raised cattle and sheep along with some hogs. We had about ten head of milk cows that we milked morning and night. The hired man and Sterl usually did the milking but sometimes they would be out rounding up cattle so the job of milking fell on Cele and me. I was just too little to do much but I did manage to milk a couple of cows, that is until I got older. We separated the milk and sold the cream to a Creamery in Arcata Bottom which had to be delivered once a week or it would be spoiled and the Creamery wouldn't accept it. The skim milk was fed to the hogs, dogs and chickens so nothing was wasted. Occasionally we would put a large flat pan of the skim milk on the back of the wood burning stove so that it would sour and get clabbered. Then we would heat it so that it became cottage cheese. Clabbered milk becomes quite thick so we used a knife to cut it up into squares which helped to release the whey.

When I was older it was my job to wash the separator, a device that separated the cream from the skim part of the milk. The separator stood about four feet high and had a large metal bowl on the top where we poured the milk that was to be separated. We turned a hand crank which rotated a series of small thin, round disks which took out the cream. Everything had to be kept very clean so the cream wouldn't sour. We kept the cream in five gallon cans made specifically for this purpose.

I never did like the job of milking. One reason for this dislike was a cantankerous cow who kicked every time we milked her. I didn't know this the first time I tried to milk her. The men always put leg hobbles on her when they milked. So, this lovely creature started kicking after I had about a quart of milk in the pail. She ended up with one foot inside the pail, and the milk that remained was too dirty to keep so the cats had an extra feeding that night. Cele helped me hobble her but that didn't stop her. She just lifted both hind feet and kicked out at me so I scrambled away from her as she continued to kick. Cele and I decided that she was one cow that wouldn't get milked that night so Cele took off the hobbles and we turned her out of the stanchion and drove her outside. We both thought that a little suffering from an over extended bag wouldn't hurt her and it might help to calm her down.

Our house was a large two story building with a fireplace in the parlor and a wood burning stove in the kitchen. A wide porch, at least 6 feet wide, ran the entire length of the front of the house and hops were trained up to the top of the posts that supported the roof. The hops lost their leaves in the winter and when spring came they grew dense and thick which kept the porch area a nice cool place to sit and sleep during the hot days of summer. We always had several beds on the porch for the children and company to sleep on when they came to visit. My aunts and uncles usually slept there.

The man that built our house and owned the property fell off the roof as he was finishing the shingling. He broke his legs and had other injuries which led to his death. He was building the home for his fiancé and was alone the day that the accident happened. He managed to crawl a half mile to the main road where he laid for quite a few hours before the neighbors found him. He was in very bad shape by the time they reached the hospital in Eureka. Dad bought the place from his estate for about three thousand dollars, which was a good price in those days.

The country was sparsely settled with our closest neighbor about two miles away. It was still quite wild and primitive as there wasn't any electricity or telephones and most of the people living on Kneeland were still traveling by horse or horse and wagon. There was a stage that made the trip every other day, stopping at a small hotel for the night. There were two hotels on Kneeland.

One was named the Fair Oaks Hotel and the other one is where Aunt Cele and Uncle Bill eventually lived. It was called the Fitzgerald Place.

All of us kids slept upstairs. There was one huge room and one bedroom. Cele and I had the bedroom and the two boys slept in the big room. Cornell didn't like to sleep there but he was four years old and should be weaned from Mom. It was hard on him for awhile and he suffered almost every night with leg aches. He would wake us all up crying so hard but no one seemed to know what to do for him. A bag of heated salt seemed to help some but it wouldn't stay warm for too long. Mom had nursed him until he was two years old so that was one reason he didn't like to be so far away from where she slept, which was in one of the bedrooms downstairs. He was her baby and she did spoil him to a great extent.

When we would go to bed at night we would open one of the windows to listen to the night sounds. We sometimes could hear the black bears fighting in the green gage orchard. The green gage plum was named after Sir William Gage and some of our English ancestors brought it to America. The wild animals enjoyed raiding the orchard when the green plums were ripe. The bears sounded like two bulls fighting which sent shivers down our spines and scared us. We could also hear a mountain lion scream if they invaded the territory. We called them panthers. Coyotes were very numerous and bold. Some nights they would sneak into our yard and try to steal the chickens. It was up to Sterl to see that the chicken coop was closed for the night. One night for some reason Sterl forgot and sure enough we were awakened by much squawking in the hen house. Dad got up and took his shotgun so that he could fire one shot near the building which scared the coyotes away. Skunks were always invading the area beneath the hen house to search for eggs. The dogs didn't pay much attention to skunks but would put up a howl if a raccoon invaded the small orchard below the house. We usually kept the dogs tied up near the house or in the woodshed which was located just a few feet from our back door. We didn't want them tangling with the coyotes.

Most of our neighbors were Irish as their ancestors had immigrated from Ireland. They raised sheep and cattle on their ranches. Due to the large coyote population the ranchers that raised sheep had a government hunter help them in their extermination process. They used poisoned meat and traps which didn't always bring the results that they wanted. Since we didn't have many sheep, it was easier for us to take care of them and out of harms reach. Each night we corralled them or put them in the barn.

The government hunters also took care of the bear and panthers that were giving the ranchers problems. Bear could kill a calf with just one swipe of his front paws especially if he was an old male bear. They and the panther would go for the throat after getting the livestock down. One big leap on the back of an animal would usually put it on the ground in a defenseless position.

Coyotes were also enemies of our turkey flock. Occasionally I would go with Sterl on his early morning jaunts through the trees and brush searching for turkey nests. Some mornings we would get up before daylight, light a lantern and sneak out of the house. We would check on the nests that Sterl had found and then search for new nests. If a coyote had invaded a nest and sucked the eggs the hen turkey would be found in the lower branches that are thick and concealing. Of course he always carried a 300 Savage gun just in case we might come face to face with the dreaded panther or bear. I can remember being scared a lot while I was with Sterl especially if we heard some unusual sound in the woods. Sterl just lived to be outside, with a gun, a lantern, and lots of courage as he was always gone from home very early almost every day. If Dad was home he would help Sterl move the turkey and her eggs to the turkey house which cut down on our loss.

We always had a pen of hogs so that Dad could make bacon, hams, and sausage. Mom would try out or render the fat from the less desirable cuts of meat and she also made head cheese from the pigs head. Lard was our main source of fat for cooking and Mom could make the most delicious apple pies and brownies. I was never much of a sweet eater when I was little so I would just sample her goodies. Dad always kept several hogs for butchering and sold the rest to a slaughter house in Eureka. One day Dad wanted to butcher a hog so he asked the hired man to kill it. The hired man stabbed it through the heart with a long very sharp knife. This didn't kill the pig. It ran squealing all over the pasture and could not be caught. It still had the knife thrust in its heart and didn't die until it had bled to death. Sterl and the hired man chased after that hog until they were exhausted. Dad was really put out with the way the hired man handled the problem.

I was the one who usually kept the fires smoldering in the smokehouse during the curing. I always looked forward to the times that the smokehouse was full of salmon as I really enjoyed eating this delicacy. Dad would saddle up Dolly (our mare) and take his spear and go down to the Mad River to fish when the time was right. Some of the salmon were as tall as a man and the steaks that Dad cut from the center of the fish were a good twelve inches long and a beautiful dark red. The most delicious food anyone could ever experience eating.

We had a large white leghorn rooster that had a real mean streak in him. He chased Cornell and me and scared the daylight out of us. Those spurs on his feet were long and sharp. When he attacked us he would fly up and try to spur us. One day he was threatening Cornell and Sterl happened to be outside so when he heard Cornell scream he ran to see what was going on. Then the rooster attacked Sterl. It was like a bolt of lightening hitting him. Sterl grabbed him around the neck and twirled him around and around until he was dead. The old white rooster neck was twisted like a corkscrew. He ended up in a stew pot with dumplings.

Mom had a neat way of cutting Cornell's hair. She put a bowl on top of his head to hold the hair down so she could cut a neat straight line across his forehead. He always had bangs and a page boy cut. His hair was about the color of bleached straw so Mom used bluing to help keep it looking almost white. Mom always seemed to pay more attention to Cornell's appearance. Sterl was just the opposite. His hair was brown and usually quite straggly so he presented quite a sight in his baggy coveralls, hitched with one bib, the other one hanging at his side. His clothes never seemed to look clean as he was always messing with skinning some fur animals and scraping the fat off from the skins.

Sterl was quite thin and small for his age but he was a wiry little person. He weighed just a little over two pounds when he was born. Grandmother Paddock could slip her wedding ring over his foot up to his bottom. Mom developed child birth fever after Sterl was born and she almost died so Aunt

Bertha Moore helped take care of Sterl for awhile. Then Grandma Paddock took over the nursing job. They fed him with the aid of an eye dropper every hour. I don't know if Mom ever nursed Sterl. Of course she couldn't when she was so ill. Grandma put him in a shoe box that she lined with soft woolen material and then put him on the oven door to help keep him warm. Sometimes she even put him inside the oven. It was quite a tricky job keeping the oven at an even temperature because the stove was a wood burner. They warmed olive oil to rub all over his body and did not bathe him except for cleaning him after he wet or messed his diaper. They didn't dress him in baby clothes so put soft woolen blanket squares over his little body. Diapers were about the size of a man's handkerchief. At night time they would light several coal oil lamps and put these around his shoe box bed which kept him warm.

As I said before, Mom almost died giving birth to Sterling. If it hadn't been for Dad she never would have lived. Dad dipped sheets in cold water and covered her body with these during the time of her very high fever. He had to do this day and night for several days until the fever began to subside. The doctors didn't have antibiotics in those days. They used laudanum to ease the pain. I sometimes wonder if Mom was afraid to get pregnant again after this life threatening experience. But she did, otherwise Cornell or I wouldn't have been born.

Cele was four and a half years older than me so I didn't play much with her. She seemed so grown up to me and I can't remember doing anything much with her while living on Kneeland. Cele stayed in the house most of the time while I liked to be outside. She liked to read and did help Mom quite a lot. Cele weighed ten pounds at birth and always remained overweight.

Cele and I shared a double bed in the large bedroom upstairs and the bed was shoved up next to the wall so I wouldn't fall out. I was also a sleep walker. One night I fell between the bed and the wall which frightened me. I felt like I was suffocating. I cried and did everything I could to try and get out of this trap that I was in. Cele didn't hear me but Mom heard the thumping on the wall as their room was directly below ours so she came up to see what was the matter. The bed hadn't been pushed tight to the wall when it was made that day. What a relief to get out of the situation.

I was always thinking up many different things to entertain myself since I didn't have any other children to play with. Sterl was usually off on his jaunts and Cornell was still taking naps and stayed rather close to home and Mom. I collected blue clay from a little stream that was just below our house. From this clay I modeled people and animals or whatever came to my mind. After modeling them I would put them on a board and leave them in the sun to dry. I collected moss, acorns and many other things from nature so I would build models of farms and houses. We never had any toys that came from a store. Everything was hand made.

Dad built a wagon for us so that we could hitch our tame goat to it. One day I was riding in the wagon with Sterl leading the goat and all of a sudden the goat decided to take off. It was a wild ride for awhile, at least until I fell out. Before Sterl could catch the goat the wagon had received considerable damage. Dad repaired it for us and put a few restrictions on how we used it. Dad also built us a cart that we could haul things in such as wood or the baby goats and sheep. We hauled each other in it too.

One summer a friend visited us who was a biology buff. He taught us how to build a butterfly net and how to preserve and mount insects. I was the only one in my family who seemed truly interested in the project. I loved to run over the hills catching butterflies. I also loved the beautiful summer days that I pursued this activity.

Most summers we had several tubercular men living below our house in a grove of oak trees. They pitched their tents and set up their simple housekeeping furniture which consisted of an army cot, a couple of benches and a table. They would rake the twigs and branches from around the tent and line a walkway with rocks that they painted white. They also used the white rocks to form a boundary around their tent. They thought that this would keep out any snakes that might invade their territory. Some of the men were quite old and others much younger. The doctors wanted to get them out of the damp weather that Eureka was noted for. There was such a lot of rain and fog. They thought that the hot dry climate on top of Kneeland might help to cure them of this terrible disease. One was a World War I veteran who told us many stories about the war. Sterling liked to talk with him and I usually tagged along to satisfy my curiosity. Tuberculosis was quite prevalent in Humboldt County. Many people died from this disease and few recovered. One of our young friends died when he picked up the germ in an abscessed tooth. It just kept eating away on the jaw bone until he couldn't eat as chewing was so painful. He became very thin and soon died.

Sterl and I loved to grab hold of a long limb on the big oak trees and swing back and forth. Sometimes we climbed quite high in order to find a suitable limb. One day I climbed into a smaller oak tree that was growing just below the house in a rock outcropping. Our out house was down near this tree and after leaving the outhouse I thought it would be fun to do some swinging. I climbed the tree until I found a limb that looked good and strong. When I grabbed the limb and swung out I fell to the rock pile below. It knocked me out and I laid there until dinner time which must have been several hours. The family came looking for me and Dad carried me into the living room and laid me down on the chesterfield. I woke up but was in a daze. I was thirsty so Dad gave me a drink of water and then he took me upstairs to put me to bed and stayed with me until I went to sleep. My head hurt the next day but I was none the less for such a fall. I guess being only five and quite small helped make the fall was less severe. After this accident I wasn't too enthusiastic about this fun activity. Sterl wasn't with me on this day as he was out checking his traps. I was usually alone since Cele didn't enjoy doing things that a five year old likes to do and Cornell was too young so I usually ended up playing by myself.

Our nearest neighbor family that had children lived about three miles from our home. The Barry family. Mrs. Barry invited us to visit her for tea one beautiful summer afternoon. Mom took Cele and me. Their little girl, Alice, was a couple of years younger than me so I was eagerly looking forward to meeting her. Alice told me that her mama cat had some baby kittens. Of course I wanted to see the kittens but when Mrs. Barry told Mom that they didn't have their eyes open yet Mom very quickly told me that I would have to wait until their eyes were open. I couldn't understand why she wouldn't let me see them. When Mrs. Berry went into the kitchen to prepare the tea she asked Mom to come with her. This gave me the opportunity to coax Alice into taking me to the barn so I could see what was so mysterious about kittens with their eyes closed. I closed my eyes and that was fine. Why couldn't kittens? The kittens were with their mother, all snuggled around her in a soft bed of hay. When I held one I thought they were so tiny and maybe they had pink eye like I had a year before and couldn't open my eyes. Then we heard Mrs. Berry calling us so Alice and I ran out of the barn real fast. Mom didn't know what we had done so I didn't get punished.

Some of our most exciting times were with our cousins. Aunt Bertha and Uncle Fred drove into our yard in their automobile. The four Moore boys would pile out and start running all over the place, exploring barns and everything else that looked inviting. When they were there all of us children slept in the hayloft in the barn. Sometimes an owl would fly in and out and let out a "whoo" which always scared me and Cornell. Since our cousins were city boys and not used to country life they were frightened when they heard the horses stomping in their stalls or heard the rustling of mice in the grain bins. Sterl got such a big kick out of them that he would add to their fright by pretending that a wild animal was trying to get up to our sleeping quarters. In order to get to the top of the hay mow we had to climb a ladder as the mow was about twenty feet high. It was easy to get down because we just slid down on our rear side. That was so much fun. Once Cornell fell off the top of the hay mow on the wrong side so he hurt himself quite bad. No broken bones though. Mom wouldn't let him go any more. We put a large canvas on top of the hay and slept on this inside a rolled up blanket.

We sure liked to have Aunt Bertha and Uncle Fred Moore visit us because she always brought lots of good food such as fresh crab and fish, usually salmon. Mom would make several rhubarb pies and a big kettle of chicken and dumplings. She also cooked green peas and little potatoes and served them in a cream sauce, slightly thickened. Yummy yummy. A large pan of home made biscuits always accompanied this delicious meal, and served with freshly churned butter. Sometimes we had honey that Dad got from robbing a bee tree. To separate the honey from the comb and a few dead bees Dad would put it in a large colander and smash it so the honey would drain out of the comb into the pan below.

Our Grandpa, William C. Paddock, taught us kids how to locate a honey bee tree. He would put some honey or sugar and water on a saucer or pan, set it outside for awhile until a bee found it. After the bee loaded up it would fly away and we would run after the bee which sometimes took us quite a distance from home. One bee was hard to follow so we would wait until several bees were working. It sure took a lot of patience and running but if we found a honey tree it was well worth the effort. I liked to chew the comb that was richly filled with the golden honey. The honey from wild bees is darker in color and the comb is quite brown compared to what we get today. Dad would build a small fire at the root of the tree if there was an opening there and smoke the bees out of their home, then he would pull the honey laden comb out and put it into a five gallon milk can. Wild bees build their nests in trees that have a hollow place in them caused by disease or fires. Sterl and Grandpa usually found the bee trees.

I loved to tag along behind Grandpa and could keep up with him as he was about 78 years old and not too well. His rather long white hair and long white beard would flow behind him if the wind was blowing. He would be holding out his arm with the honey dish in his hand and would be singing some old time Civil War songs. It was a pleasure to see this tall, large man walking and singing as he walked thru the bushes in search of a bee tree. Grandpa was over six feet tall and muscular due to his many years doing blacksmith work. We loved him very much. I guess because he was such a happy jolly man. I never did see him angry no matter what happened.

If you ever find a bee tree you must wait until night time when it is good and dark, to rob it. The smoke helps too. Sometimes Dad would cut the tree down and split it open in order to get the honey out. Bees aren't active at night time.

When Grandpa would get tired he would sit down on a log or stump of an old tree. I would sit with him and listen to some of his stories about the Civil War. Grandma wouldn't let Grandpa go alone into the woods for fear that he might pass out. He suffered from Ague which he got while serving in Andersonville prison as he had been caught by the Southern Army. So after Grandpa came home from the Civil War he wasn't very well. The Ague left him with something like epilepsy. Ague is a fever usually caused from mosquito bites. One of us children always went with him on his walks which were every day and sometimes several times a day. He sure liked to walk through the woods. I enjoyed being with him very much. He was a grand old man. Recurring high fevers and chills with lots of shivering left Grandpa weak and many times he would blank out. I only saw him in this condition 2 times. It happened once while Grandpa and Grandma visited us on Kneeland. Us kids went for a walk with him and when he became tired he sat down on a log to rest. He became blank in his expression and didn't talk to us. He seemed to stay this way for a long time before he woke up. I would say it was as if he was in a trance. Another time Grandpa and I were alone in the living room and he was standing over the wood stove warming his hands by rubbing them together over the heat. All of a sudden he landed over and both hands fell flat on top of the hot stove. I yelled for Grandma and then I tried to hold his hands up off the stove. Grandma was there in a flash so between the two of us we could hold him up until the spell passed. His hands hurt for several days but he didn't get third degree burns. Grandma always appreciated having some of the grandkids around to watch Grandpa just in case he had a spell. He didn't start having these spells until he was an old man which was a blessing as he was a blacksmith and they use fire every day.

Sterl and I would spend the summers hiking all over our ranch. I guess that Sterl covered it more thoroughly than I did but I did quite well keeping up with his pace. We would stick a couple of dry biscuits in our pockets just in case we got hungry and didn't make it home for lunch. We drank sparkling clear water from the streams that ran through our ranch and would eat water cress that grew along the banks of the stream. We also ate wild mustard, blackcap raspberries, huckleberries, and wild strawberries when they were in season.

Our herd of angora goats lived on the Red Knoll most of the time which was quite a distance form the barnyard, maybe about a mile. It was Sterls and my job to check them a couple of time each week. The old billy goats had such long twisted horns that would occasionally get caught in the thick shrubs and they couldn't get loose. I was afraid of them because of their horns. One old goat had horns that were a foot long and they stuck straight out on the side of his face. They looked like giant corkscrews to me. Their wool was long and curly and usually snow white. Their wool brought a good price during the World War I as the Army liked to buy socks and sweaters made from it. It wore well and was warmer that a lot of other materials. I haven't seen a herd since and am wondering if they have become extinct.

Cele usually stayed in the house reading or helping Mother while Sterl and I and sometimes Cornell would climb in the wagon and go with Dad and the hired man to the fields. We would ride on the scrub that was used to pull over the ground after plowing so that the seeds would have a smoother surface for growing. It was fun and helped weigh the scrub down. We also loved to ride home on top of a load of grass hay as it was so soft and smelled so good. Dad also raised oat hay. We had two large barns near the house which had to be filled with hay. This barn was about a mile from our home. It was used mainly by our horses who wintered there. It burned down one night and we believe that a convict who ran away from prison was sleeping there, as we found an old agateware coffee pot, cup and some twisted spoons in the ashes. We didn't find any bones so never knew if the man survived the fire. Dad and the sheriff examined the area really well. I'll never forget the day that Sterl discovered the burned out barn. Dad wasn't home and we hadn't seen the fire but some friends from Eureka told us that they saw the fire and wondered what it was. It had a lot of hay stored inside so it must have been a very hot, fast burning fire. Maybe the man burned to death and was like a person cremated. A mystery that no one ever solved.

Getting the hay stored in the barn was quite a big job. The hired man would stay inside the barn on the pile of hay and Dad would remain outside on top of the wagon load of hay. He used large metal pincers like giant jaws which would grab a huge amount of hay and then Dad would use a lever to make the jaws close tight around the bundle of hay. This gadget was called a fork lift.

The hired man would stay inside the barn and scatter the hay round. Dad and Sterl would stay outside to put the large hay fork lift into the pile of hay that was in the wagon. Our team of horses would then pull the hay up until it reached a door at the top of the barn and it would catch onto a track which carried it to the far end of the barn or dumped anywhere along the track. The hired man would yell to let Dad know where he wanted the hay dumped, then Dad would pull the tripping rope. Once a huge fork of hay fell on my Dad and Sterl as they were standing beneath it. Somehow the fork got tripped accidentally as my father was teaching Sterl how to drive the team. They both scrambled out of the pile of dusty hay coughing and blowing something awful. Sterl was about fourteen years old, and Dad wasn't well as he had had a couple of strokes so he wanted Sterl to take over this job.

The great horned owl that I mention in a previous paragraph was always a fascination to Sterl and me. Sterl would light a lantern and take me with him to investigate the owls habits. We would get as close to the corner as possible and try to shine the light from the lantern into the owl's eyes. There were fewer mice and rats due to the old owls nocturnal habits. He lived there for about three years but one day he was missing and never did return again. Things like this added a little excitement to country living.

One beautiful summer day my two brothers had gone for a walk which took them about a mile from our house. On their meandering walk they passed thru scrub oak trees, down animal trails, up little hummocks and through hazel nut bushes continuing on until they came out into an open space. Cornell was only 3 ½ years old, quite young to be tagging along behind an older brother of eight years. Sterl was a very alert boy and was always keeping a sharp eye out for wild birds or animals. All of a sudden he stopped and gave Cornell a signal to be very quiet. Beyond them on top of a knoll was a large cat with a very long tail. Sterl recognized it immediately as a mountain lion or cougar as we called them. The cat was leaving the opening and heading for the forest so he did not see the two boys nor did he smell them. Sterl grabbed Cornell by the arm and pulled him along toward home at a fast pace. I'll never forget how excited he was when he tore into the house yelling for Dad. Fear drove them like the wind. Cornell stumbled a couple of times but Sterl pulled him up and kept on running. Cornell was too frightened to even cry out when he fell, but the minute he saw Mom he started to cry with tears beginning to stream down his face. He just couldn't comprehend what it was all about. Sterl was so exhausted and panting for breath that he had a hard time making himself clear to Dad what had happened.

Dad got in touch with the government hunters so they brought their dogs and other equipment to our house so that they could prepare to search for the cougar. During their search they ate and slept at our house. Each evening after dinner in the shadows of the oil lamps the men would talk for hours about their exciting hunts over the past few years. I'd crawl behind our old wood burning cook stove and listen to these exciting stories. They made me shiver but I would eventually fall asleep and Dad would carry me upstairs and put me to bed.

I'd awake in the early hours of the next morning to the hustle and bustle of the hunters preparations for the days hunt. Mom would give them a filling breakfast of pancakes, thick sliced bacon and eggs which they washed down with strong brewed coffee. Sometimes she served hash browned potatoes which always went over with much appreciation. Since it was dark, daylight was a couple of hours away so the men each took a lantern. We didn't have any flash lights then. The dogs had been fed and leashed and were showing signs of excitement as they seemed to anticipate the coming hunt. Of course the men had cleaned and polished their powerful rifles the night before so that they were already for the big hunt. The cougar population was very high in the Kneeland area when we moved there. They killed a lot of sheep, young calves, and deer thus the need for government hunters.

My Uncle Marion Paddock told me a spine tingling tale of a cougar that trailed him for several miles. Uncle Marion had killed a young buck deer and was carrying it home on the back of his horse. Sometimes the cougar would get ahead of him and then slink behind. Sometimes the cougar probably smelled the blood of the deer and it must have been quite hungry. Uncle Mary, as we called him, was prepared to shoot the cougar if he could have gotten a good look at him but due to the thick growth of shrubs and trees, the cougar was hard to see. As Uncle Mary came out onto the open prairie the cougar faded away and didn't continue his stalking.

Kneeland was quite a primitive area when we moved there so as we got older Dad taught us how to shoot and handle a gun safely. Sterl was a very good shot when he was ten years old and had even been hunting when he was younger.

When summer arrived I was always eager to seek out the wild strawberry patches. Cele, Sterl, and I would take little tin pails and go to the areas where the berries grew the best. Many of the berries were as large as marbles, luscious with the rich sweetness of wild strawberries. It didn't take us very long to fill our small pails as they grew very prolific on the south slopes of the prairie. We would take them home so Mom could make us delicious strawberry shortcake that she served with the thick cream that came from our dairy cows. To this day I don't think I have ever tasted a more delectable strawberry shortcake. Sometimes our wild berry picking took us a mile away from our house so Sterl always carried his 300 Savage rifle along just in case a bear or cougar would attack or threaten us.

The first birthday party that I attended was given by our nearest neighbor lady for her little girl, Alice Berry. Alice was several years younger than me but we still had fun being with each other. In order to get there Dad let me ride our horse Dolly and he accompanied me riding another horse. Alice's home was built way down at the bottom of a large hill which was about two miles from our house. They also had another home for winter use which was closer to the county road that ran along the top of the prairie and ended at the Cosgrove ranch. Since she had a summer birthday her folks were living on the lower ranch and that is where the party was held. Just Alice and me made up the party. Alice's mother sent us outside to play while she finished getting the treats ready for this small celebration. With nothing much to do I decided to march around the house with Alice following and I started singing a little ditty that I had learned form some of the older children at school. It went like this "Oh the Irish and the Dutch, They don't amount to much, but the Irish beat the Dutch". As far as I was concerned the song didn't have any specific meaning to me but when Mrs. Barry heard me teaching this song to Alice she got real mad and took Alice inside and spanked her with a hair brush. I felt real bad and when Alice returned outside with tears running down her face, I hugged her. We didn't sing anymore but did continue to drum on the pie pans as we marched. Years later I learned that Mrs. Berry was Dutch and her husband was Irish. I was never invited to another birthday party at Alice's home.

When Alice started first grade in school her Dad made her ride a huge horse. We usually met her at our gate which led to the county road and accompanied her to school. She was such a tiny little girl and we really felt sorry for her. Most of the time she would be crying when she arrived at our place. We walked the mile to school most of the time unless it was raining or snowing. Winter arrived early the year that Alice entered first grade. One weekend in November it snowed about a half foot so when Monday morning arrived we had to don our boots and trudge through the snow. When we got up to the county road we were so surprised to see Alice sitting in the snow beside her horse. She had fallen off and of course was too small to climb back on. The poor little thing was so cold and frightened and crying up a storm which didn't seem to disturb the huge old mare. Sterl ran down to our house to tell Dad that we needed his help. Well, Dad picked Alice up and grabbed the reigns of her horse and took her down to our house. After he got her warmed up he saddled his horse and took Alice home. I believe he gave Tim, Alice's father, a very severe talking to concerning letting such a small child go alone to school in such bad weather. Thereafter someone always rode with Alice until she reached our place.

Life for all of us soon settled down to the usual daily routine which kept us all quite busy. Each child had daily chores to perform, some more, some less, depending on our ages. Cornell and I carried the split chunks of wood into the house and dumped it into a large woodbox next to the kitchen range. When the box got low on wood Mom would send Nellie, that's what we called Cornell, and me to fill it up again. One day when we got outside Nellie refused to help me so I picked up a length of wood and hit him on the arm. He started screaming as loud as a four year old can scream so Mom came running outside to see what the problem was all about. I started crying because I thought that I had really hurt my brother. Mom gave me a good scolding and gathered Cornell up into her loving arms and informed me that I would have to carry all the wood for awhile until I learned how to behave. Mom sure babied Cornell.

Whenever Sterl or I would get under Mom's skin she would send us outside which seemed to me to be a lot of the time. I guess I always managed to get into some kind of trouble. Once Mom sent me to the hen house to get some eggs because she wanted to bake a cake. I filled the small pail and on my way back to the house I managed to fall and break half of the eggs. When Mom saw the eggs all covered with broken yolks she was really upset and gave me a good dressing down. Another time when I was six years old I took my turn washing the dinner dishes which I didn't want to do so I told Mom that I would break all the dishes. I didn't really mean this but for some untold reason I did break a glass and the broken glass had cut my hand so when I showed it to Mom she got real mad and sent me to my room for several hours. She pulled the curtains and made the room dark so I couldn't play. I laid there until dinner time, thinking mean thoughts about Mom.

Sterl and I never did seem to receive much attention or affection from Mom. Dad always seemed to treat us about the same, always kind and understanding and any little problem that we had was his problem. Dad was gone from the ranch a lot of the time because of his business which was buying and selling cattle for the slaughter house. When I look back on this part of my life I realize that it was a difficult period of time for Mom, especially with Dad gone so much of the time. We always had a hired man whom Dad instructed to help Mom whenever she needed help. He helped with the laundry each week by carrying buckets of hot water to the wash room and even ended up scrubbing some of the clothes such as overalls. He wasn't too impressed with this line of work. He didn't mind chopping the heads off the chickens and cleaning them because he surely enjoyed Moms chicken and dumplings. When we were short on meat, the hired man would go deer hunting which he was pretty good at spotting a young buck deer. All of us tried to help Mom by gathering fruits from the orchard, vegetables from the garden and pick strawberries from the berry patch. We also had blackberries and Logan berries which Mom made into jellies, jams, and pies. The hired man also helped Mom can hundreds of quarts of fruit. Cele helped some, me too, by pitting cherries or peeling apples. I could peel apples good because we had a gadget that would peel as I turned the handle that ran a blade around and around the apple. That was fun, but pitting cherries to make pies wasn't much fun. The others were canned with the seeds in tact.

Another chore that was given to me was churning butter. The churn was like a round wooden tub with a tight fitting lid which was suspended between two ends of framework. It had a handle on the right side that I would turn around and around until the butter solidified. When I thought that the butter was made I would take the cover off and look to see if I was right. Once I accidentally tipped the churn and out flows the butter and buttermilk onto the floor but I did manage to upright the churn and save some of it. Another one of my messes.

I believe the sink in the kitchen was made of galvanized iron and the faucet above it only ran cold water as we didn't have a hot water tank at that time. Hot water for our baths had to be heated on the stove. When bath time rolled around, usually two or three times a week, we filled a large galvanized tub with water and took turns in the bath. Nellie, then me, next Sterl as he was usually the dirtiest. Cele always bathed alone with clean water since she was the oldest and quite the young lady. My sister developed quite early as she was only ten when her periods began. I believe this led to a great deal of heartache for her a couple years later.

My hair was certainly not my crowning glory when I was little. Someone told Mom that if she would shave my head it would grow in thicker so that is just what she did. Dad wasn't too keen on the idea but he went along with her plan. After Dad cut my hair I must have looked like a shaved convict. I hated it so would hide if a neighbor dropped in for a visit as I was ashamed to let them see me looking like a scalped "banshee". Mom finally made me a cap to wear so I wasn't so self conscious. It took a long time for my hair to grow to its original length and the shaving didn't thicken it up either. Actually it was thick but quite fine.

In the spring wild mushrooms popped up everywhere. Dad taught us how to distinguish the good ones from the bad so we would take our pails to the thickest patches and have filled in no time. Mom would dip the larger mushrooms in egg and then roll them in cracker crumbs before frying them in some of our sweet home made butter. They were so good and everyone in my family enjoyed having this delectable treat.

When the apples were ripe in the fall Sterl would sling a gunny sack over his shoulder and hike over to the old Foss place where he found an old orchard that had been abandoned. He could fill the sack about half full of those delicious red apples and bring them home for all of us to enjoy. One trip by Sterl wasn't enough to satisfy our appetite, so he would make several each year or until all the apples were gone. His picking competed with the deer because they liked apples too, and there were hundreds of deer on the prairie. We stored our apples under the water tank which was built on top of a tall structure that resembled the old windmill towers. Water from the tank would leak over the sides and splash on the ground which helped to keep it cool. We also kept our milk, butter and other perishable foods in the storage area beneath the tank.

Sterl and I loved to go into the water tower storage area to cool off when the weather was very hot as the cool, dripping water would spray over our heads getting us slightly damp which felt so good. Of course we enjoyed munching on any food that was stored there. Sometimes we would get a scolding if we had consumed too much of a certain food. We especially liked the sauerkraut and deer mincemeat. Mom was a very good cook and she liked to entertain people so whenever anyone came to visit she usually had some type of dessert to serve. So you see she didn't appreciate having any of us children getting into her stored food.

During the summer months we had plenty of fresh fruit such as wild strawberries, blackberries and huckleberries. When we moved to our Kneeland ranch there were apples, pears, and plums. Mom made plum butter which was so good on biscuits and pan cakes.

In order to preserve eggs for our winter cooking we made a thick white solution, called water glass. The eggs were stored in this liquid in a large pottery crock and they were used primarily for cooking and baking.

Sometimes Sterl and I would sample the green gage plums before they were ripe and as a result of this we often got a stomach ache. When this happened I usually crawled behind the wood burning kitchen range and curled up until I felt better. This is where I would be found whenever I didn't feel well. I had a lot of problems with my stomach. Many foods gave me pains so I assume I was allergic to certain foods. If any of us children had an earache or tooth ache we would heat a sack of table salt in the oven of the wood burning stove. The heat seemed to relieve the earache or tooth ache.

Sterl and I went barefoot much of the time in the summer. Cornell and Cele didn't pursue this activity very often but would accompany Sterl and me if we were going to do some wading in the small creeks near our house. There were also many little springs of water on the ranch. Some of them trickled away to form small streams that meandered down the mountain side to join larger streams. These were the spots that drew us away from the house especially during the hot summer days. We loved to wade in the water squishing the soft silky mud between our toes. Of course we were always looking for frogs, wire worms, and I think polliwogs topped the list of creatures that we discovered. Sometimes we would carry an old tin can or jar along so that we could capture a creature to take home to show Mom and Dad. Mom hated some of the things that Sterl captured, especially the small garden snakes.

When I was eight years old we were still living on our 340 acre ranch on Kneeland Prairie. I really loved this period of my life. Mom had divorced Dad.

Dad hired a woman teacher, who taught at the little one room school, to live with us so Cele, Sterling and I would have someone to help take care of us. The teacher's husband and little girl also lived with us. I remember being jealous of the little girl as she was about my age, and she was always very prettily dressed with shiny patent leather sandals. I usually went bare foot during the summer. Those beautiful shoes made me feel so inferior and the only dresses I had were hand-me-downs so I didn't hang around the house very much. The hand-me-downs weren't all that bad but I still felt that the little girl looked at me with distaste.

Usually I roamed the hills during the summer time when we weren't going to school. All of the wild animals, birds and other living creatures kept me fascinated as I enjoyed just watching them. I especially enjoyed the beautiful blue birds and loved to listen to the blue-jays chatter.

Sterl set traps to catch chipmunks which he put in cages that he had made so I had fun feeding them. Sterl also set traps to catch raccoons and baby quail. I could sit for hours watching and talking to these animal friends. I never was lonely for company.

About the only chores that I had to do was gather the eggs and haul in wood for the kitchen stove. Sometimes I churned the cream into butter. Occasionally

I did some milking if Sterl and the hired man were gone. I didn't consider herding the turkeys a chore because I enjoyed following them all around the ranch. They fed on wild oats, grasshoppers, and other seeds that were available. The little turkey bells that the gobblers wore would tinkle so merrily as they strutted along leading the flock of hens. Sometimes a hen would sneak off in order to find a good nesting place for the eggs she would soon be laying.

While watching the turkeys I would collect moss and gather acorns from the scrub oak trees which I used to make play dolls and houses. I'd bring the flock home late in the afternoon before the sun set. Sometimes they didn't want to go home. I'd have to run this way and that trying to bunch them up. Once in awhile an old gobbler would chase after me strutting and gobbling like mad. It would scare me and I'd have to back off. I soon learned to carry a branch from the oak trees so I could shake it in his face. This worked real well.

There were some huge boulders on our ranch. One was just below the house and was almost as tall as a two story house. All of us children loved to climb to the top and look around and since it was quite flat and covered with moss we would lay down and take a nap if we were tired. Usually the naps weren't long because the sun beating down on us would make us too warm for comfort. Near the base of the big rock was a small spring from which a trickle of water flowed down over a hill. The soil above the spring was good and had quite a large flat area so Dad planted a garden there.

We hauled water from the spring to water the garden. Instead of eating any lunch I would pull a carrot or two, some small beets the size of marbles and shell a few peas which satisfied my hunger.

When the school term was over, the teacher and her family who were living with us went back to Eureka, so we were without any one to help us cook. Dad tried to keep a hired woman most of the time. Being isolated as we were, that was a problem.

One housekeeper had an affair with our hired man who was about ten years younger than her so Dad had her pack her bags and he took her over to the old Fair Oaks Hotel to put her on the stage. Then Cele did most of the cooking with Dad's help but Dad was gone much of the time. We ate a lot of beans with deer jerky cut up in chunks and stewed with the beans. Not bad at all. Cele made lots of pancakes and rice pudding with raisins. Sterl shot many wild rabbits that we roasted in the oven.

If we cut ourselves or got a scratch we'd wash it with some strong soap like Fels Naphtha and that's all we did. Occasionally a cut would get infected then we would soak the wound in a pan of hot Epsom salts solution, lancing it with a sharp pocket knife would let the wound drain. We also used a Lysol solution to disinfect wounds. A few drops of oil-of-peppermint would help ease a bad stomach ache.

My dad, Garf Paddock, was called out many a night to help doctor the children of neighboring families. A distraught parent would come galloping his horse at a break neck speed to our farm yard. This noise and the wild barking of our dogs would get us out of bed to see what was going on. The Fulton family seemed to seek Dads help more than any other family. Mrs. Fulton was a young wife and mother and a town girl to boot and very inexperienced. They lived a good four miles away so Dad had to saddle up our favorite riding mare, Dolly, and follow the scared father to their ranch. This constituted a full nights work as Dad would sit up with the child until it became calm and stopped crying. Usually the child had a fever or was colicky. Traveling by horseback at night was bad, especially when there was a foot or more of snow on the ground. When there wasn't any snow the trip was easier as Dad could follow the narrow winding road over hills and down the mountain sides. It surely helped when the moon was full. If there was no moon, the brilliant stars seemed to give off a lot of light. When you were on top of this mountain range, it seemed like the stars were close enough to reach out your hand and pluck them off. Such brilliance I've never seen since. I think it was because the air was so pure and crystal clear.

The Cosgrove ranch was about three miles from our place. They often had Dad come over to doctor their sick animals. One night around three o'clock we awoke to pounding on our front door and a young boy's voice screaming and yelling for someone to open the door. At this time we only had one dog, Spot, who knew the young Tommy Cosgrove very well so Spot didn't bark. One of the Cosgrove's prime mares was trying to give birth to a foal and had been in labor for a very long time. By the time Dad got there the mare had just given up and had very little life left in her. The foal was so twisted up inside the mare that there was no way she could give birth in a natural manner. So Dad had to perform a cesarean operation to deliver her baby colt. The colt survived but its mother couldn't make it.

Previous to this Dad had performed a cesarean operation on a doe deer that a hunter had shot and wounded. The doe was almost dead when Dad found her and he could see that she was heavy with her babies so he cut her open and removed two little fawns. Then he had to kill the mother. Both the fawns survived.

Another problem that the Kneeland ranchers had to contend with was the dreaded larkspur and wild hemlock. Dad was frequently called upon to help save these stricken animals as gas built up in their stomachs and they bloated. One method was used which required a long sharp knife that was thrust into the stomach between some ribs which let out the accumulated gases from the stomach, then the men would insert a smooth stick of wood in the opening to keep it from closing up. Larkspur and Hemlock liked warm, damp places to grow so was usually found near spring or streams. Most of the ranchers fenced these areas but occasionally a cow would break through the fence to get to the lush green food. This usually happened during the summer when the grasses were dry and yellow.

Sterl and I had the job of checking our cattle to see that they didn't break into these isolated areas. One day when I was checking the cows I found that three had broken out and were eating the dreaded plant. It wasn't the tops that caused the trouble. It was the roots which were easily pulled out of the wet soggy soil. Those darn cows wouldn't budge for me so I had to find a limb that had fallen from a tree to beat at them in order to make them move. This was quite frightening for an eight year old because the place that they were in was very brushy and soggy with water and logs and the area where Sterl and Cornell had seen the mountain lion. I was afraid to yell at the cows because I thought the cougar would hear me. Well, as it was, I ended up screaming and beating at them until they gave up and left with me tailing behind giving out a string of yells as I beat at anything I could find that would make noise. After I got them with the rest of the herd I high tailed it for home to tell Dad.

Dad, Sterl and the hired hand saddled the horses and rode out to round up the herd and bring them home and keep them corralled until the fence was mended. One cow got sick but didn't die so that pleased me.

Most of the fences on our ranch were made from oak poles and several strings of barb wire so the animals seeking greener pastures would keep leaning on the wires, stretching their necks further and further until a post would fall down. In the pastures where we kept our herd of sheep we used American wire. Sometimes we'd find a sheep with its head caught. Usually we found them before they would die.

One day our black sheep dog got hung up in the sheep fence near the top and when I found him he was almost dead. The poor thing was hanging there with his tongue hanging out and blood oozing from one cornier of his mouth. The reason was that his neck was being squeezed by the wire. His big eyes were pleading with me to get him out. Since I was quite small I didn't think I could handle him so I ran for help. Dad was home so he dashed out with me following at his heels. after Dad released him from his strangle hold he just lay there on the ground all flat and stretched out. I though he was dead. Dad told me to run and fetch some water. Dad gently dribbled some water of the dogs tongue which helped to revive him but he had no desire to get up so Dad said "We'll leave him as he is and he'll get up when he's ready". Sure enough, about five hours later he came to the house for his dinner. I gave him a couple of biscuits soaked in milk. I can't remember his name but he was one of our prize sheep dogs.

We had some of the most sought after dogs in the entire mountains. We raised a litter of pups every year. The mother was also black and she always had about eight to eleven puppies that were black. Most of them had a patch of white below their mouths. Dad could train and teach them to do many things on command such as "go left, go right, stop, circle, heel", and some commands I have forgotten. Dad got a thousand dollars from a man who had a thousand or more sheep. Usually they sold for around one hundred dollars.

The worst thing that happened to me when I was eleven years old was a rattle snake bite on the calf of my right leg. Dad had promised me that he would take me hazelnut hunting the next time he came home so he kept his word.

We started off on a beautiful sunny day just slowly ambling along, enjoying the pleasures of each other and the beauty around us. Dad wasn't too well since he never got completely over his accident of the head injury from the falling tanbark tree, so we didn't hurry.

It was the Fall season so there were lots of leaves beneath the trees. Dad had carried a four foot stick which he used to bring down the taller branches. Hazelnuts grow on a bushy shrub, sometimes eight to ten feet tall.

I was walking in front of Dad as we entered the patch of hazelnuts. The gray squirrels had beaten us to many of the nuts so Dad said, "we'll go into the thicket growth and hope to find more. So far we only had a handful. All of a sudden I felt a sharp jab in my leg. I turned my head and looked at Dad and said, "you jabbed my leg with that stick", which had broken in half just prior to this. Dad said "no I didn't". Then as I took another step I cried out and said, "Dad, you stuck me again". Dad said, "I threw the stick away". We walked about fifty feet arriving at an open place and then I fell down flat on my face. Dad hurriedly knelt down and looked at my leg. He saw two puncture wounds about one-half inch apart so he knew what had happened.

Dad took his jack-knife out of his pocket and opened it to the small thin blade. Then he told me to lay real still because a snake had bitten me and he had to lance it to get some of the poison out. I laid real still and thought more about the snake coming after us again so did not feel too much pain when Dad cut a cross shaped slice over the two punctures in my leg. Then he quickly sucked the wound, spitting out after each suction. He did this for a few minutes. Then he took a leather shoestring from his boot and tied it around my leg above the knee. Dad carried me home. This happened in August, just after my 11th birthday, and it was the time of year snakes go blind during the skin shedding season.

After we got home Dad put me to bed and gave me some medicine. I don't know what he gave me. Dad stayed up with me all that night. He gave me milk to drink when I was thirsty. I was in sort of a stupor all that night so don't remember all the times I vomited. Dad later told me that I vomited the milk and it was very dark and clabbered. The doctor told Dad that this probably helped get out some of the poison. The next morning Dad had the hired man hitch up the team onto our flat bed wagon so I could be taken to the stage that stopped at the Fair Oaks Hotel which was about four miles from our ranch. We didn't have a car at this time which was the 1920's . The stage was a Ford passenger car.

Dad sat up front with the driver and another man. The driver put me in the back with two ladies. They were dressed so fancy with feathers in their hats and frilly white blouses and shiny black shoes. All I could do was stare at them.

We had only gone a few miles when one of the ladies said, "We can't abide sitting by this sick child. We'd prefer having the gentleman sit back here". So the driver stopped, got me out of the back with Dad's help and put me in front between him and Dad. Then he told the two ladies what he thought of them. The rest of the twenty five miles was made in almost total silence. The stage driver took us directly to Dr. Falk's office when we got to Eureka.

The driver was still sputtering to Dad as he helped get me up to the doctors office. I'll never forget those two hoity-toity ladies and their repugnant behavior toward me and Dad. One of the ladies said, "I'm afraid she'll vomit on us". I was happy to be transferred to the front seat so I'd be close to Dad.

I spent about a month recuperating at my Great Auntie Poyfaire's house. I was in a comatose condition for about two weeks during this time. I remember nothing. My two Aunts took care of me as well as my second cousin, Del Merritt. Dad helped out too.

Dad told me that our very special Dr. Falk came to see me every day. The first thing I remember when I came out of the drugged state was my Dad, Aunt Florence and Dr. Falk standing around my bed, and I heard Aunt Florence say, "It's the strangest thing, she just lays there with her eyes open but there is no expression in them". After that I improved quite rapidly except for a large swollen leg that was red with white and black spots all over it. I thought my leg looked huge and that surely worried me. I was afraid the doctor might have to cut it off.

After a couple of weeks the doctor told me I could go home so I was a very happy girl. After I went home I had terrible dreams about snakes. I could smell a bad odor that seemed to come out of my pores as I was still a little feverish and having night sweats. The odor was so repulsive and I often thought that it must have smelled like a snake pit. In time this passed.

That Autumn I entered school as a third grader. Sterl was in fifth grade and Cele was in the seventh. Cornell was living in San Francisco with Mom. We walked to school which was a mile from our ranch. Cele was the school janitor as she was one of the older pupils. Sterl and I usually went barefoot when it was warm weather but Cele always wore button top shoes or high topped lace shoes. We carried sack lunches which usually consisted of left over pancakes or biscuits or sometimes we only had deer jerky.

It was always an exciting time when Dad came home bringing oranges, candy and doughnuts along with other foods. Our meals were much better when we had a house keeper which wasn't too often at this time. We ate a lot of potatoes and gravy that Cele could cook.

On one side of our house next to the woodshed we had a covered in porch where we did our laundry and took our baths. All water was heated on the kitchen stove. There was a cold water faucet over an old steel sink so we didn't have to go outside for cold water.

When Cele, Sterl and I kept house we managed to keep fairly clean but we didn't iron many clothes. We just hung them on the line and let the sun and wind help make them presentable. Sometimes Cele would heat the sad irons and press some of her dresses. We also had flat irons that had a detachable, wood handle. They were kinder to our hands.

After Mom left us we never had much company. The men from other farms came to see Dad and occasionally they would bring their sons. All would ride up on their horses, with the boys pulling their mounts in to a sudden stop. They were showing off their riding skills.

I can remember one boy in particular. Charlie Hunter was his name. He never got off his horse but just sat there like a lord looking us kids over. He was dressed in a riding habit that looked like it might have come from Paris. Compared to how we looked he was a prince. He was about Sterls age, ten years old. Sterl and I invited him to get off his horse and come play with us but he declined in almost a grown up way. Guess Sterl and I didn't appeal to his better senses. Sterl had on his usual attire of bib overalls, with one strap dangling as usual and we were both barefoot.

Charlie's folks were well to do and his mother kept him as clean as a whistle.

Their ranch was about 20 miles away. His Dad and hired men had come to take some cattle back to their place which they had bought from Dad.

Years later Charlie became a friend to Sterl. He had some movie stars from the series "Rawhide" staying at his place for the hunting season. Sterl was one of the best shots in the mountains. He was good at rounding up cattle and as a young man he was in demand when an extra herder was needed. Charlie Hunter found Sterl as a reliable friend and maintained his friendship until he died.

As soon as the first heavy snowfall arrived in the winter, school would close for a couple of months. Being snow bound was a happy time for us. We spent much of each day outside stomping trails through the snow which usually was three feet deep. The trails we made meandered this way and that way ending up at the milk house, the horse and cow barn, the sheep barn and the woodshed. One winter the snow was so deep I could run through the labyrinth of trails without anyone seeing me as my head was below the snow line. I remember several winters when the snow completely covered the fence posts that ran along the road. Our ranch ran along the ridge of Kneeland Prairie so when the wind blew fiercely it would pile the snow into deep drifts which no beast or man could negotiate. All animals were kept inside the barns.

One winter night the snow arrived earlier than expected and by morning we had a foot of the beautiful white stuff. Our herd of sheep were still out on pasture. We knew we'd have to get them inside as soon as possible. We hurriedly got dressed in our winter clothes, and tore out of the house without a thought of breakfast. Dad wasn't home and we knew this is what he would want as he had taught us well. It is very hard for sheep to survive in the snow as the snow balls up on their wool coats and weights them down. Then they flounder around and get on their backs and can die, especially if they are heavy with twin lambs, which our ewes were. It was afternoon before we got them all inside. Many of them had to be pushed, shoved, and almost carried in order to move the herd along. By this time we were starving hungry. We hurried into the kitchen for a good pancake breakfast that Cele had ready for us. After eating, Sterl, the hired man and I went back to the barn to pull out the snow balls from the sheep's wool. We fed them some hay and filled their drinking trough with water.

Our herd of Angora goats were much smarter than the sheep. We seldom brought the herd into the ranch compound. They were more like the wild animals so when a storm came up they would hi-tail it to the shelter found beneath the tall fir trees that grew thickly over a third of our ranch. Their diet was mainly from browsing on the thick underbrush of the forest. If the winter became too severe we would load some hay on our sled for the goats and we let the horses do the pulling.

We sold the wool from the goats to the Eureka Woolen Mills where it was woven into material and used to make socks and other items of clothing for our World War I veterans. The goats wool was very warm and durable.

One winter day before Mom left, Sterl coaxed us to go for a walk with him to the lower barn which was a good mile from our house. It was all down hill to the barn so the going was a breeze for us. The snow was frozen hard which held us up so we didn't break thru. Sterl filled the mangers full of hay and cracked the ice on the water trough and removed most of the ice. By the time we headed home the sun had warmed us up considerably. It was a beautiful sparkling day. We felt so happy and just loved our day of freedom from the house. By the time we got near the top of the hill the ice crust began to break up and our legs would break thru. In two feet of snow we were floundering around, our feet and legs got wet and very cold. My shoes kept coming off because I didn't have them tied well. I finally took them and my socks off and carried them. My feet were so numb I couldn't feel much pain. Cele's stride had carried her well ahead of Sterl and me and she didn't give us any help. Sterl kept trying to help me. By the time we reached home we were so cold and wet. This happened when I was about five years old. It was the year before Mom left.

Mom got a tub of warm water, took our clothes off and put us in the tub. I was first as I was in the worst shape. Cele and Sterl kept their shoes on so they didn't suffer so much. They did get a good scolding from Mom.

One of our favorite pets was a reddish colored dog with white spots so his name became Spot. Spot would follow us to school every day. He made friends with the other children and fared well during the lunch hour because many children gave him scraps of food. He would lay beneath a window or on the little front porch patiently waiting for the school day to end.

Many of our neighbors were of Irish descent. At first they weren't too friendly, especially our nearest neighbor. They raised sheep and didn't take too good care of them. Overgrazing caused a lot of problems because their fences were so poorly constructed which gave the sheep an opportunity to push into greener pasture. There were a lot of coyotes on Kneeland prairie, so many sheep were killed by them. Our neighbor, Tim Berry, accused us of letting our dog run wild to kill his sheep. Our pet dog, Spot, was the culprit according to Tim. So Dad paid him for several sheep, and told us to keep Spot chained, which we did. Then again Tim said he lost some more sheep to our dog. We knew better because Spot was tied up. Tim insisted that he saw our dog chasing his sheep, so Dad thought we had turned Spot loose. Dad told us that we would have to kill Spot because we couldn't afford to go on paying Tim for the dead sheep.

Dad had the hired man shoot Spot. That took place while we were in school. We loved Spot so much because he was a loving and friendly dog. We always felt protected when he was with us. When we got home from school Dad showed us where they had buried Spot. We cried a lot over his grave and planted wild flowers on the freshly turned sod. We lost our good pet and constant protector and it took a long time to get over this loss.

About a week after Spot's death, old Tim came to our house again stewing mad and accused us of letting our dog kill more of his sheep. When Dad told him that he had shot Spot, Tim pulled in his horns and finally admitted that it must have been the coyotes killing his sheep. We kids never forgave Tim for what he had done.

When spring arrived the following year, Spot's grave was a mound of green and later on wild flowers bloomed again. Our dear pet was gone forever. We mourned him anew and missed him so much. I think Sterl and I missed him the most because he was always tagging along on our excursions over our land. Cele stayed in the house much of the time and Cornell had gone to live with Mom.

I don't remember ever having a kitten for a pet but I do remember a neighbor giving us a cat soon after we moved to Kneeland. That cat spent most of its days living in and near the barn where we milked the cows. They would squirt a stream of milk into the cat's wide open mouth and then fill a dish full of the foamy milk. There were lots of field mice in the barn so I guess the cat preferred that home to one nearer to us.

Mother was a very good cook even if she only had a wood stove which seemed like a black monster to me. Above the stove top there was a warming oven that kept the food good and warm. The warmth from the old black stove was surely welcomed during the cold blustery winter. Now summer time was another problem. Sometimes it was just too hot to cook. If she wanted to bake bread or some goodies she usually did it right after breakfast.

The men liked a sumptuous meal in the early morning before beginning their daily chores. We had a large cast iron pancake griddle that would cook eight pancakes at once. This was the usual fare but occasionally we would have biscuits, and almost always eggs fried in bacon drippings. Once in a great while we would whip up a batch of waffles. The waffle iron was also made of cast iron. When we used it we would remove a lid from the stove and set the waffle iron over a well stacked bed of coals. We often burned our hands on the two long iron handles which were used for turning the gadget over so the top side would get browned. But the effort was well worth the trouble. Especially when we had good thick cream to spread over the waffle and then a thick layer of sugar was added. Yummy.

World War I was still raging so some foods were very scarce. A coffee substitute that Dad made consisted of wheat and molasses. He baked this mixture in the oven until it was brown and crisp. Then Dad ground it in a coffee mill as fine as possible. It made quite a tasty brew. Tasted something like the Postum we can buy now. Of course we added some rich cream and sugar as desired by each of us. It was a good hot drink for winter days.

I was in first grade when Mom left us. I enjoyed school, although I didn't learn much in the first and second grade. I was the only first grader for most of the year. Then Annie Gray joined me. She was from a family who moved to the mountains for the seasonal logging of timber. I will never forget how she would pull up her dress and blow her nose on her petticoat. It gave me a sick feeling. Annie's family was so very poor. She had five brothers and sisters. In time Annie and I became good friends and she graduated with me from eighth grade. The county health nurse taught her family about cleanliness and gave them some good clothes so their outlook on life was better. One of her brothers and a sister died of tuberculosis. For most of the school day, Annie and I would look at pictures, color and whisper to each other. Sometimes the seventh and eighth graders would try to teach us phonics and help us read.

Annie and I shared a little table that faced a small slate blackboard which we practiced writing our ABCs on. The first letter I learned to write was an "S" because one of the older girls told me it looked like a snake.

We had thirty eight pupils at this time. We had one teacher, Miss King. Some of the students were quite old for grammar school. We had about five boys who were sixteen to nineteen years old. The older boys gave the teacher a lot of problems as well as the younger children. One day they pestered several of us first and second graders by making us walk down some large planks and spit on the planks as we walked. If we didn't spit enough they would yank our hair and call us names. I almost hated them as they laughed at us. They would "guffaw" in class at lots of us. They could see everything that went on in class because they sat in the last seats in the room. Those boys were always "smirking" and pulling off some practical joke, like putting a few firecrackers in our large pot bellied wood stove. Some of these older pupils left school but new ones seemed to always replace them.

Many of these new students had migrated with their parents from the Eastern states like Oklahoma and Tennessee. To me, one of the worst things they did was to a little seven year old boy who was retarded. His last name was Snow. He came to school each day with his sister who was about a year older. They always brought a couple of sandwiches for lunch. One day at lunch time these "hooligans" as we called them, to ourselves of course, got the little Snow boy behind the large pepperwood trees and took his pants down and made him urinate on his sandwiches. He was so scared of them and so retarded that he complied. Then they tried to force him to eat the sandwiches. When they did this, the younger kids yelled at him not to eat his sandwiches. "You'll get sick, you'll die".

Several of us rushed into the classroom to tell the teacher. She stopped the ruckus and sent the little boy home with his sister along with a note. The school board met and decided that the Snow boy shouldn't attend school any more. Soon after this, his family moved away and I never heard any more about them.

At the end of each school year, the pupils always put on a program for their parents. I remember having to learn a little poem while I was in second grade for the program. It went like this:

"Little birdie hopping on a window sill,
Cocked his shining eye and said,
Aren't you shamed
You little sleepy head."

Was I ever nervous with all the parents watching. I made a mistake so started all over again. That time I remembered it all and acted out the part. Another program that I participated in was, "Dance of the Angels". We had to do a simple dance step and hold out our arms to simulate angels wings. I was eleven years old and the smallest one in a group of five girls. Our dresses were all made by one of the girl's mother as she had a pedal sewing machine.

My dress was a pretty bright pink. The other girls wore blue, green and white. The seamstress took a length of cloth and doubled it so it would come down to just below our knees. The sleeves were left very large and hung down almost to our waist. When we held our arms up and rotated them it was supposed to resemble an angel in flight.

Most of us were quite clumsy dancers so the audience laughed at us. The music to accompany our dance came from the school Victrola. One had to wind it up by hand. The teacher didn't wind it up too much at the last so we would droop like tired angels. When we did our drooping dance the parents just howled with laughter.

After the children's program we had games and contests such as sack races, ball throwing, ante-over, foot racing and baseball. By this time the teacher and mothers had the pot luck food laid out on plank tables put up on saw horses.

The food, especially the home made ice cream, was scrumptious. One of the fathers would take his Model T Ford to Eureka to get big chunks of ice and rock salt for the ice cream making. Some of the parents brought two-quart jars full of the vanilla ice cream mixture. It was enough to fill several hand crank mixers.

Large galvanized tubs were used to freeze the containers of ice cream. Gunny sacks were soaked in water and put on top of the tubs to help keep the ice form melting too fast after the ice cream was frozen. This was a super treat for all the mountain people. Usually the only time we had ice cream was during the winter months when we would collect icicles and ice from the tops of the watering troughs.

Other delicious foods were hams, fried chicken, potato salad, sandwiches, and oodles of sweets like cake, pie, cookies and puddings. Some of these women were outstanding cooks and when we had a gathering like this they really tried to outshine each other.

Usually we had four weeks of summer vacation, but it could be shortened depending on how severe the previous winter was. Winter vacations lasted for two months.

Sometimes Dad would hitch up the team to the wagon and take us to school if it was storming. He had a canvas that he would stretch over the wagon bed. There wasn't very much head room, about 14" high. We'd crawl under the canvas so we wouldn't get wet. Dad or the hired man, whichever one took us, would wear rain slickers and rain hats to keep dry. They also wore hip boots. Some days, if the storm was rain, hail, or sleet, the horses would balk at having to make the trip. If Dad wasn't home, the hired man would balk as much as the team did so we would end up staying home thus often missing many school days.

Cele was the janitor during her eighth and ninth year of school. After a pupil finished eighth grade they could continue going to school for another year. The school board paid Cele a small fee for her work. She had to haul buckets of water from a little spring about a half mile from the school house. When we wanted a drink we would use the long handled dipper that was kept in the bucket. All of us drank from the same dipper. Cele also cleaned the slate chalk boards and swept the floors, put the toilet paper in the boys and girls outdoor privies, and dusted the furniture and window sills.

Some of the older boys started wasting the toilet paper by throwing it down the hole. They even sneaked into the girls toilet and did the same mean trick. After that the teacher kept the tissue paper in her cloak closet and had a monitor give it out when needed.

The boys toilet was at one end of the play ground and the girls at the other end. We sometimes experienced harassment from the older boys as they sneaked around behind the girls toilet and used cat calls to scare us.

After Cele finished eighth grade, the teacher took over the janitor work for awhile. I got the job when I entered my sixth grade of school. They raised the pay to ten dollars a month which was quite a lot of money for a child to earn. Hauling the water was about the hardest part of the job except for cleaning the ashes out of the pot bellied stove. During the cold weather my hands would get so cold as I didn't have mittens, and had to still carry buckets of water. We used some of the water to wash our hands before lunch if they were dirty. We used an old tin basin and a towel on a roller that was located in the back of the room on a wooden bench. I did the janitor work for three years, my sixth, seventh and eighth grades.

After I graduated from 8th grade, I would go back to school and work as a teacher's aide. I enjoyed helping Mrs. Bassford with the little children. I didn't spend as much time with her as I wanted because Dad needed me to drive him around the country to many farms where he bought cattle. Dad suggested that I use the money I earned to buy calves from a Portuguese dairy farmer that we knew. He helped me buy about 5 little heifers to raise. I branded them the summer I was 15. I had branded them myself with Dad's branding iron. Sterl helped me by holding them down. If our cows weren't giving enough milk to feed my calves, I used powdered milk that we bought in 25 pound bags. All the income from these calves was going to be mine so I guess I took extra special care of them. I had ten calves when Dad died. They varied in size and ages and were all Guernsey

Irene Paddock and her Guernsey cattle

heifers. The law wouldn't let me keep them as they considered them part of Dad's estate. My hard earned investment was divided up between the four of us, Cele, Sterl, Nellie, and me. and I never did get to sell them at an auction. All the livestock was sold after Dad died.

One of my most embarrassing moments at school was when my union suit flap fell down as I was writing on the black board in front of all the classes. I was wearing quite a short dress which I had really grown out of and the back flap came unbuttoned and dropped down. The kids could see the bottom edge of it hanging below my dress hem. I heard snickers all around me. I dropped my arms and just froze. I forgot what the teacher asked me to do so I guess she figured that I didn't have the ability to solve the problem so she excused me. When lunch time arrived I just sat in my seat and wouldn't budge until every child was out of the room. Since this was a beautiful sunny day all the kids took their sack lunches and sat beneath the large tan oak trees so they could enjoy the shade and each others company. The teacher always sat at her desk to eat her lunch so when I didn't get up out of my seat she asked me what was the matter. When I explained, she had me come up to her desk and she used two large safety pins to repair the flap so it wouldn't fall down again. Later on in the day I had to go to the toilet. I managed to unfasten the pins but couldn't get them fastened back so the flap wouldn't sag. I was gone so long she sent an older girl out to see why I hadn't returned to the classroom. Cele wasn't in school that day or she could have helped me. Union suits were a one piece garment that was an under shirt and pants all woven in one piece. The girls suits had the flap at the back that buttoned with two buttons, one on each side. Now the boys suits had one long slit opening which was much more convenient. When I got home that night I took off that suit and put on an old worn out suit that had been Sterl's which he had outgrown. I had a great feeling of satisfaction and freedom from having a no-flap under garment on. I wore Sterl's old suit to school the next day and no one knew. For a few days when the teacher wasn't around, the kids teased me and called me "droopy pants". Soon something else came up to take their attention.

I was only eight years old and had no one to teach me how to sew. I couldn't repair my clothes. I tried but the big stitches never held very well.

Soon after this the teacher asked me if I had anyone at home to teach me and help me sew. When she found out that I didn't have anyone she brought needles and thread to school and supplied all the younger girls with cards that had small holes punched in them so we could learn to knot the thread and sew in and out of the cards she made and some outlines she had bought that had designs and outlines of animals or flowers which we had to follow.

My Dad had a very bad accident in the woods. It happened one beautiful spring day in 1923. He had hired a man to help our hired hand fall some timber. Dad went over to see how they were getting along. It was a strict custom to yell out "timber" just before a cut tree fell. This day they didn't do it and my unsuspecting Dad walked into the area and the falling tree hit him. It split his head with a very severe gash, severing an artery. Dad almost bled to death. His life after the accident was never the same. For a long while he was very pale. I thought he was as white as a sheet, and he was so tired he could hardly move due to the loss of blood. I loved my Dad very much and tried to help take care of him. I'll always remember how I sat on a log with him one sunny day and gently held his hand. His body craved the heat of the sun so he would sit for hours absorbing the warmth of the sun. Mom wasn't happy during this time. I guess she was already thinking about a divorce. Dad seemed so sad too.

Mom invited her sister to come for a visit the next summer after Dad's accident. She was Mom's foster sister and had been living in San Francisco. We called her Aunt Alice. Aunt Alice's Mom and Dad took my Mom in and raised her like their own daughter. This was after my Grandma Fulmore had a nervous break down which was caused by the disappearance of her husband Charles Fulmore, my grandfather.

We heard so many stories about Grandpa Fulmore's disappearance but this is the one we believe. He went to Canada to search for gold and never came back home. No one heard from him. He had just vanished. Many people searched for him. There is a stream or creek in Canada named Fulmore. My Mom's brothers, sister, and other relatives believe that Grandpa Fulmore was killed. Probably he had found gold on this stream bed. Many miners were killed for a gold discovery.

When Mom's foster sister came to visit us that summer she talked Mom into piercing Cele's and my ears. They used a needle that had been sterilized over

Charles Fulmore and Amelia Bowden Fulmore

a hot flame from a coal oil lamp. Mom held a cork from a bottle behind our ears as Alice jabbed the needle through the ear lobe. Then they put a string through the holes and tied a knot so we couldn't get it out. I didn't like this at all so I got a pair of scissors and hid behind the barn. It took me a long time to finally sever the string and yank it out. When Mom saw what I had done she was sure put out with me. They threatened to put the strings back in so I ran outside and far away into the woods. Alice told Mom to let me go and that I was probably too young to appreciate it.

A few days after this both Mom and Alice were gone along with Cele and Cornell. Dad was gone so Alice really worked on Mom to convince her to go to San Francisco with her.

I knew something was going on that I didn't like and I was scared. Mom, with Alice's help was sorting and packing clothes and putting them into suitcases.

Some man from Eureka picked Mom, Cornell, and Alice up at the ranch house the next morning and on their way out they stopped and took Lucille out of school. Of course all three of us had gone to school as we usually did during the summer months. She left Sterl and me in school. I wanted to go with Mom too. I put my arms around her and cried and she shoved me away. She told me to go home with Sterl after school. She said Dad will be home soon. Sterl and I were alone at Kneeland and it was several days before Dad got home. Our nearest neighbor was three miles away. I'll always remember the day she left.

Dad was away on a cattle buying trip to Hyanpaum creek where the Indians raised cattle for their livelihood. The Indians always liked Dad and trusted him as he never cheated them on a deal. On this trip he would be gone for about two weeks.

When Mom left, Sterling and I were all alone as Dad had taken the hired man with him. She didn't plan for being gone thus the food supply was really low. All I can remember having to eat was biscuits, dried deer jerky and some fruits and vegetables from the garden. Since Sterl and I were only about six and eight years old we surely didn't know much about cooking. In those days everything was cooked from "scratch".

While Sterl and I were all alone we stayed close to the house. We had the dogs to help protect us and kept them near us. It was scary at night especially when we would hear a cougar howl or a couple of male bears fighting.

The coyotes howling would send shivers thru my body and I'd "scrunch" down inside the covers. I was so thankful to have a brother who always seemed so brave, and he really was. Sterl at the age of eight already knew how to handle a gun and shoot almost as good as the men.

When we ran out of food the men killed a pig, deer, goat, or chicken for meat, or when the rabbit season was on they would go out at night and spotlight the rabbits which made them easy targets. Rabbits weren't good eating during the hot summer months as they would become diseased. If a rabbit had any "boils" on its body, it was discarded or cooked and fed to the dogs. I never enjoyed eating the rabbits and only did so when cajoled or forced to do so.

Sterl was trapping at this age and had a string of traps during the winter months that covered quite a large area of our 350 acre ranch. He never left the house without a gun slung over his shoulder. When he would go to check his traps he draped an old gunny sack over his shoulder and back, a good way to carry home the animals that were caught. Sterl skinned all the animals that he caught and scraped the hides to remove any fat and then he would tack them to the side of the barn so they would dry. It wasn't unusual to see the stretched tight skins all over the side of the barn. To help keep the flies off the skins, he sprinkled alum and salt over the surface of the hides.

Of course Cornell and I were curious spectators to this skinning ritual. We also learned about the inside parts of an animal like the liver and heart.

After the animals were skinned, the remaining carcass was cooked outside and given to the dogs for their dinners. We didn't have dried or canned dog food in those days.

Now I am going back to when I was five years old and had the chance to observe a spectacular phenomenon. In Eureka we had a total eclipse of the sun. My family and I were visiting Grandma and Grandpa Paddock at their Eureka home. Dad told us that it would get as dark as night and we would have to light the oil lamps. Dad smoked some pieces of glass so we could look at the eclipse thru these so that it wouldn't hurt our eyes. We were so excited. Especially my brother, sister and me. We cavorted around the yard and house in anticipation of having night time during the day.

Some of the people in Eureka were religious fanatics and had been preaching that the end of the world was going to come and begged people to pray real hard so they would go to heaven. They held a revival meeting in the park and stirred up some of the people to quite a frenzy. I remember some people crying and slapping their hands on the ground and praying to God.

Well we waited for the world to come to its end and waited to see darkness in the daytime. I was real scared but Dad reassured me that the world wasn't going to fall to pieces.

As the darkness slowly began to descend on the earth, Grandpa's chickens went into their coop to roost and the few turkeys they had in a pen gobbled, clucked and ran around like crazy. The wild birds flew to their nests in the trees and when it got total darkness the stillness of the animals and birds was sort of eerie. It made me shiver. It was rather strange to witness the quieting effect that the eclipse had on everything. It didn't last very long. Soon all the noises of the animals began to be heard again.

The second total eclipse I witnessed was February 26, 1979 in Othello, Washington. I won't be on this earth when the next one rolls around in 2017 but my children and grandchildren and great grandchildren should have a chance to see it.

I have tried to keep my life history according to each year but I find this is very hard to do as I never kept a diary.

The summer after Mom left home we had revenue officers from the federal government spying on our activities. Someone had reported to them that we were running an illegal whiskey still. They would sit in their cars for hours just watching. We kept our eyes on them and Sterl tried to do some counter spy work. Of course all of us kids stayed mighty close to home since we feared these strangers but the chores had to be done like milking and feeding the cows. One day Sterl crawled around the hill until he was out of their sight and he sneaked up quite close to them. When he got back to the house and told us that they had guns leaning on the car fenders we were really frightened. Also there were four men and Dad was gone on a trip to Eureka with our hired man so there were just three of us home. One day Sterl said, "I'll give them something to watch". So Sterl went out in our front yard and acted like a child possessed by the devil. He turned hand springs, stuck out his tongue, and ran his hands thru his hair to make it stand up. Cele and I laughed a lot. The revenuers left every night and returned the next morning, usually at first light. We never did know where they were staying. After about a week of spying on us they got out of their cars and all four of them headed for our house carrying their guns. We were sure scared and didn't know what to do. We thought they were going to kill us.

Sterl was the brave one so he said, "I'll go out to see what they want". He took his 300 Savage with him. He stood in the front yard with the gun in his hands, almost as quiet as a statue. The four men slowed their pace and yelled to Sterl that they just wanted to talk to us and wouldn't harm us. One of the men handed his gun to the man nearest him and proceeded down the road to talk with Sterl. Then out of curiosity Cele and I went out on the front porch.

Sterl was only 10 years old but he acted like a man as he told the revenuer to go ahead and search. Sterl followed them all around the homestead, into the barns, woodshed, chicken coup, and they also covered a good portion of the woods below our house. The men used pitch forks to jab all through the hay. All they found was a small bottle of Sterl's cider that he had hid in there. They left and never came back to our house.

One of our friends, Eddie Baxter, did have a moonshine still way back in the rugged mountains. Since Eddie always stayed at our house on his trips to town to buy supplies, we thought that was the reason they searched us. Many of the Kneeland people knew that Eddie produced some good whiskey.

Uncle Bill James and Sterling went to see Eddie one beautiful spring day. They rode their horses into the front yard of Eddie's cabin and were met with a gun blast from a shot gun. As the story goes, the horses reared up in fright. Then Eddie aimed the gun at them until he found out who they were.

Eddie's small shack was built beside a mountain spring that gave him sufficient water to run his little business. It was located about five miles from the nearest dirt road. It was far back in a mountainous section of the Iaqua hills. He used an old deer trail to transport his supplies by horseback to the cabin.

Every now and then Eddie would get the urge to associate with people. Especially the girls from Second Street which was Eureka's red light district. He fell in love with one of the girls and asked her to marry him. My Dad helped Eddie arrange the wedding. It was a simple wedding at the Justice of the Peace office.

Since Eddie didn't have a car, Dad took him to town in our old model T Ford. Just before they left Eureka, Eddie and his new bride shopped for food and some other necessities for keeping house. New sheets, pillows, and blankets were at the top of the list. Eddie had left his riding horse and pack horse at our house when he hitched the ride to Eureka with Dad.

Eddie and his bride spent the first night of their married life at our house. Dad took Cele and me aside and told us that we should treat Eddie's wife with kindness and respect even if she was a woman of ill-repute. She had mended her ways. We always listened in on adult conversations whenever the opportunity presented itself. We wouldn't think of hurting Eddie as we liked him a lot. He had an exciting personality. He was very cheerful and full of fun and spent time entertaining us.

He was what I would call a cute man. He was short, thin, with sparkling brown eyes and his hair was getting thin at the temples.

The next morning Dad loaned Eddie two horses. One for his bride and one for packing their things. Sterl saddled up his horse to go along so our 2 horses could be returned to our ranch. Eddie wanted to buy one of our horses but Dad told him that he needed them soon for a cattle round up.

Eddie asked Dad to find him a young, gentle mare for his bride. When Dad was in Hyampaum he found just the right horse for Eddie's bride.

Eddie made a very long V shaped trough to carry the mash down the mountain side. His still was quite large so he had a lot of mash to get rid of. The chipmunks, gray squirrels, and other little animals fed on the mash so there were lots of drunk animals. I never did get to see Eddie's layout but Bill James and Sterl told me about it. The revenue men never did find Eddie's still. They came mighty close a couple of times. It was said that he made fine whiskey. Much of it was sold in Eureka and some in San Francisco on the black market. Eddie built his bride a new house nearer to civilization. Eddie died quite young—due to drinking his own moonshine.

I will never forget the old man from Germany who visited us quite often. He would bring his Stradivarius violin and play sweet music for us. I especially enjoyed the Red River valley. I would crawl behind the old wood burning kitchen stove and listen. It was a warm and snugly place to enjoy things going on in the kitchen. The old man worked for a neighbor but would get lonely for companionship. We would feed him and give him a cot to sleep on. He had immigrated from Germany when he was a young man. He told us many stories about his native land and the struggles he encountered in his adopted country. He became quite sick and knew he didn't have long to live. The last time that I saw him he gave Dad his violin. He had brought it with him from Germany. It was the only thing he had from his homeland. Dad was like a son to him and he treated us like his grandchildren. We liked him so much and when he died soon after this we were so sad. I cried a lot. I would go behind the barn and sit and cry for our dear friend that we would never see again.

Our hired man stole the violin and a 38 revolver and went to San Francisco where he sold them to a pawn shop. Dad had fired him because he had beaten one of our horses with a club. Dad traced the violin and gun and found the gun but the Stradivarius violin was gone. Someone knew its value and snatched it up. Probably the pawn shop owner. Dad never did locate the violin. The violin had a number inside it that I remembered for a long time but it eludes me now.

Dad ran an ad in the San Francisco Examiner, a Hearst newspaper, for a few months but he never got an answer. Today that violin would be worth thousands of dollars. When I think about it I can visualize someone playing Dad's violin, our loss, their gain.

Mom never wrote to us after she left home, but one Christmas when I was 7 she sent me a doll that had a broken finger that had been glued back on. It was a beautiful doll and the first one I had ever had. Christmas was coming in a couple of days, but I sneaked a look at my present from Mom.

It was the only time that I saw my doll because our house burned to the ground on that Christmas Eve. The large woodshed next to the house and a hay barn below the house also burned.

Cele smelled smoke in the night and investigated where it was and she woke all of us (Sterl, me and the hired hand). Dad wasn't home. The fire started in the chimney in the upstairs area. Dad had bought a new cook stove and the hired man put it in place. He was careless and didn't get the chimney put together correctly. Since it was Christmas Eve we had built a very hot fire so we could pop some corn and make fudge candy. These were our only treats for this holiday season. Cele made the fudge. Sterl and I helped by shaking the large iron skillet to keep the popcorn moving so it wouldn't burn. The handle of the pan got very hot even with the use of a heavy pad. To keep our hands from getting too hot we would shake just a little while and then turn it over to the other shaker. Cele would melt a lot of home made butter to pour over the bowls of snow white corn. We three kids were trying to put some cheer in our lonely lives on a snowy Christmas eve. The hired man didn't help much as he was about twenty one years old and didn't feel any excitement in celebrating our way. Of course he enjoyed eating a lot of the goodies we made.

Our home was gone and we stood in the snow in our nightgowns and bare feet while we watched the flames eat away at everything we had accumulated. Nothing was left but ashes and the skeletons of stoves, iron beds, and chimneys.

Thirty miles away in Eureka, the people saw the flames shooting high in the night sky. Our neighbors saw them too so many of them came to see if they could help. Cosgroves took me home with them. Cele and Sterl and the hired man stayed in the little cabin below where our house had stood. We were thankful it didn't burn. We lived in the cabin until Dad had Uncle Billy build us a four room home. It was an improvement over the cabin, built simply with bare walls and floor with no sink or running water inside. A faucet was hooked up outside on a small porch. It was miserable and cold when we had to go out for a bucket of water during the winter months when the ground was covered with two or three feet of snow.

After our big 2 story house burned down, our little 4 room, 2 bedroom house seemed so small so during the summer months I slept outside on an army cot. Cele and I shared a bedroom and Dad and Sterl had the other one. I preferred sleeping outside during the warm summer days. I used a blanket to make a 2 sided tent to give me some privacy. Many mornings I would wake up with water dripping on my face from the blanket tent. During the night the Humboldt fog, a very heavy fog, would roll in and put a wet covering over everything. It was like a drizzle or light rain. After the sun came out to drive the fog back to the ocean, my bedding would dry out and be ready for my sweet dreams. Sterl slept outside too. He liked the hay in the barn where he threw down a canvas before he made his bed. A pillow and a couple of

Paddock ranch house that burned in 1924

blankets is all he ever used. If the night was too hot he would sleep outside under the stars. We sure missed the long front porch on our old house that was covered with hop vines. This is where we slept in the summer before our house burned.

The only flowers I remember growing in our yard were some Amaryllis. They grew about three feet tall and were beautiful bright pink. I always looked forward to see them bloom so I was the one who watered them. Some were taller than me.

Before our house burned there was a high picket fence surrounding the buildings. When Cornell was home he would climb the fence and walk along the top which was only about four inches wide. This scared Mom very much so I was assigned to watch him. For a three year old he sure could climb and get into a lot of trouble.

I always wanted to learn how to skate and ride a bicycle and so did Sterl. Dad brought home an old bicycle but it didn't have a brake that would work. Sterl tried to fix it but didn't succeed. He managed to handle it fine without a brake. When I tried to ride I soon found myself laying on the ground in the center of the dirt road. Of course I got a few bruises and scratches from the gravel but I never again tried to ride the bike. To this day I never learned how. As far as skates go we didn't have any surface smooth enough for skating. I would often stay with Dr. Fountain in Arcata. He had a step daughter my age and she had skates. She wanted to be kind and share them with me. I tried and tried to stay upright on those skates but found myself on the hard cement most of the time. Well I soon graduated to one skate thinking that would help. I learned to operate that skate like you would a scooter and it was fun.

Dr. Fountain's wife was good and kind to me. She was his second wife. His first wife Susie died during child birth. I always felt that his new wife didn't know very much because of an episode concerning a chicken. She wanted to cook the chicken for our dinner. In those days chickens were purchased from the market with their feathers plucked but the entrails were still inside. She cut the head and feet off and washed the bird thoroughly but didn't know how to take out the entrails. She asked me if I had ever cleaned a chicken and would I help her. I had cleaned lots of chickens by the age of ten, so I did help her.

When my 9th birthday was near Grandma Loena Paddock asked me what I wanted. I eagerly told her that I would like a red straw hat with cherries on it, plastic cherries I presume. Somehow Dad found out from someone that I wanted a hat. Lo and behold I received two hats. Just alike. One hat from Grandma and one from Dad. I wore those two hats wherever I went. I guess they made me feel grown up. One windy day I was searching for the Angora goats and a strong gust of wind caught my hat and carried it into the tops of some tall trees. I could see it but couldn't get it down from such a high place. I waited for another strong gust of wind, hoping it would be blown down. That didn't happen so I went home disgusted and sad. The next day I went back looking for my hat but it was gone. I never did find it. I really took good care of my other hat and after that I didn't wear it while I looked for the farm animals.

It seemed like I played more with the boys at school than the girls. I was never dressed too spiffy and felt that some of the girls snubbed me. When Frances Mullen (who later became Cornell's wife) started to school she latched onto me as her friend. She was quite a wild little girl and a died-in-the-wool tomboy. She said that her Dad would bite the ears of his mules if they didn't behave. Frances spent most of her early years helping her father with the outside chores. He was a strict individual and cussed a blue streak when things went wrong. Franny, as we called her, took up his language and rough ways. The first time she saw me she grabbed me around the middle and swung me around in circles. She was two years younger but about the same size as me. I was so startled when she grabbed me but when we fell to the ground we laughed and laughed. We became good friends after

William Cornell Paddock and Frances Mullen

that. I remember one time she asked me for the two oranges I had in my lunch. I didn't get oranges very often so I didn't want to give them to her. She stuck a deal with me by offering me a plain gold ring that she wore on her little finger. I always admired her ring so we made a trade. The ring burned up when our house burned.

Our little one room school was surrounded with huge pepperwood and tan oak trees which gave us lots of shade when the hot days of summer arrived. The shade helped make it pleasant when we went out to play. Games that we enjoyed were ante over, hide and seek, tag, soft ball, keep-away, and visiting with our friends. One day Lorna and Frances Mullen and I just wanted to talk so we went to the far side of the play ground. We didn't want the other girls tuning into our conversation. Franny liked secrets and she liked to shock me and especially her cousin Lorna. We didn't even know the word sex but Franny, being a rancher's daughter, loved to discuss the breeding of animals. One day she asked Lorna if she knew the difference in boys and girls bodies. Lorna said boys had bigger and longer toes and larger hands. Since Lorna was an only child she didn't have any opportunity to observe a boy. We didn't enlighten her but I didn't like the way Franny laughed and laughed because I could see that it embarrassed Lorna by the flush of her face. Lorna's folks protected her from observing sex and reproduction of animals. With Franny and me it was just a very normal occurrence and we never gave it a second thought.

Front of the old Kneeland School—Irene Paddock just right of left post and Sterling Paddock second from right post.

I gave up playing softball because some of the big boys threw the ball too hard. Once it hit me in the center of my throat. I fell over backwards and had a terrible time trying to breathe. It sure scared the teacher and older boys. The teacher gently massaged my throat which seemed to help. After some time I was able to get up but was sort of dizzy and staggered a little. The teacher thought I should go home for the rest of the day. She wanted Sterl to go with me but I said I could go by myself, and that is just what I did. I took my time getting home, stopping to rest a lot along the way. I sure had a sore throat for a few days.

I will never forget the day that our teacher caught several of the boys and me burning ants in an old rotten log that laid next to fence that was the boundary line for the school property. We got a good "dressing down" and each of us got slapped on the palm of our hand with a thick heavy ruler. We also had recess privileges taken away for the remainder of the week. That was the only time I ever had to be disciplined in that manner. Of course I was just an onlooker while Charlie Kidd did most of the ant burning. He also furnished the matches. Charlie tried to get the log to burn but it was too damp to cause any big fire. The other two boys helped him while I encouraged them to get rid of the ants. They were the big red ants and they sure could bite. Their bites could sting something awful. We really thought we were doing something good for everyone. One of the younger kids had an opposite opinion so she told the teacher what mischief we were performing.

After Mom left us, school was about the only social function that we participated in. Since Dad was a member of the school board we usually went to every picnic or school program. In those days there were only three school board members, and sometimes only two. Dad did most of the work ordering supplies. Our district didn't have much money so our supplies were few and the text books old and quite ragged. Sometimes the Superintendent of Schools would visit. He usually came once a year. He supervised the 8th grade graduation tests. That was always an exciting day for us. Having a visitor was most unusual. The teacher really coached the eighth graders so they would pass the civics and other tests. She was glad to get rid of some of the older boys who were trouble makers so she worked with these especially hard.

After eighth grade graduation, several of the eighteen year old kids would ride their horses at a gallop up and down the road in front of the school shooting off their pistols. They were trying to impress the young teacher. She was only around nineteen years old. Miss Dillon had her problems with these older boys. One day they locked us out of the school and they stayed inside giving her a very difficult time. She reported this to the school board. Dad got the boys parents together along with the boys and the other two board members and read them the "riot" act. There weren't any more problems after that.

During our two week vacation in the summer I would get on our horse Dolly and ride over to the post office to get the mail. The post mistress usually had candy bars to sell to the kids. If I was lucky I might have a few pennies or a nickel so I would buy candy. For five cents I could get a Hershey chocolate bar. I didn't eat many sweets so I would usually share with Sterl and Cele. It was such a great pleasure to ride Dolly because she was a very gentle horse. Dolly was the colt that Dad had given us when we lived at the Fountain Ranch in Trinity River Country. She was a very loving and gentle horse and all of us loved her so we took special care of her. Since we had raised her from a colt, she was a part of our family like the friendship between people and their pet dogs.

When I was still 14, Dad asked me to ride Dolly to Eureka which was 35 miles away. First I had to go find her as she was turned out to pasture. I took a rope with me and planned to ride her home. When I found her in the lower pasture which was about a mile away. I heard her snicker a greeting to me. After I put the rope around her neck I led her to a barb wire fence. I thought that I could put one foot on the middle strand to help me get on her back. As I put the weight on the wire it snapped and cut a 5 inch long gash in my leg. Blood started flowing and running down my leg. It wet my riding pants all the way down to my ankle. I just pressed it hard and that helped to stop the bleeding. The rip in my pants gave me some concern as I didn't have many clothes. Most of my clothes were hand me downs or made over from things given to me. I sure had trouble getting on Dolly's back.

Riding Dolly along the ridge of the prairie was exhilarating. It gave me a freedom and a spiritual feeling to be able to look at the beautiful countryside. I could see Eureka and the Pacific Ocean on a clear day. I could look in the opposite direction and see some of our neighbor's farmsteads nestled among the huge oak trees and mountain valleys. I could see the redwood forest to the south and high mountains covered with fir trees to the north. It gave me such a good feeling to be alive and part of the spectacular earth. I think I was in love with nature and with all things of equal value.

A great treat for us was when Dad would bring home large peppermint candy canes. They were about ten inches long and an inch thick. We didn't break them into pieces like most kids do. We would get a glass of cold milk and use the candy cane as a sucking instrument like a straw. It sure took a lot of sucking to get the milk to come up through the cane. When we accomplished this we enjoyed the delicious milk flavored with peppermint In order to get this to work we first sucked on the end that was in the milk which softens the candy cane.

After Mom left Dad sold some of the timber on our place. It was cut into "bolts" and then split into stoves for barrels. The loggers lived on timber. We converted the milk house into a cabin for two of them. The milk house was just below our house situated between the house and the barn.

Sterl and I enjoyed visiting with the loggers. Sometimes we liked to pester them so when Halloween came we fixed up screech cans by using large empty cans with both ends cut out. We attached a very long string through a nail hole in the side of the can. A knot held the string in place. We used bees wax on the string so that when we ran our fingers over it, it would squawk. It sounded something like two tom cats fighting. We waited until they were asleep before we began our trick. It didn't take long before they were cursing and throwing things out the window to stop the awful noise. We did this at several intervals until the foreman lit a lantern and went outside bare footed and in his white union suit, cursing a streak of very profane words as he searched behind the cabin. Sterl and I hunkered down behind some bushes and kept very quiet. The foreman stumbled over the taut string and found our screech can. Sterl and I tore out of there very fast. The next morning the foreman approached Dad about our shenanigans. Sterl and I had made ourselves scarce but we heard everything that was said. We had orders to stay away from the cabin while the loggers were occupying the building. It was some time before the rift with the loggers was mended. On one of their trips to town the foreman brought back some treats for us and explained to us why they were so mad. He said he had done a lot worse things when he was a kid. After all, it was Halloween.

Freshwater Creek ran about a half mile below our house. We wanted a place to swim so Cele, Sterl, the hired man and I dammed up the creek. We filled gunny sacks with dirt and used limbs from the fallen trees to help hold back the water. It worked very well giving us a pool about four feet deep. It was deep enough for swimming. The loggers also enjoyed swimming on a hot day. I learned how to swim with a little coaching from the loggers.

After our home burned and while living in the cabin we had a little pet pig. It was the runt of the litter. We called it "Pinkie" because it was white with its pink skin showing through. We loved to play hide-and-seek with Pinkie. He would follow us all around the rooms in the cabin, squealing as he ran. I fed him with a bottle until he was big enough to be turned out with his brothers and sisters and eat regular pig food. When it came time to remove Pinkie from his people home he didn't like it at all. In time he did adjust to the outdoor pen and gave up his crying as he made new pig friends.

One day Dad left the hired man with Sterl and me while he went to Eureka to try and get Mom to change her mind and come home. She refused so Dad offered to build her a home in Eureka and stay with us kids. Another refusal.

At the divorce trial in the court house in Eureka, the judge awarded Cele and Cornell to Mom. Cele was there so she fought Mom and the attendants. It took two men attendants to subdue Cele. She scratched and kicked and tried to get away because she wanted to stay with Dad. The judge said to take her to the convent.

Cele was put in a large room with many other girls. They slept on cots lined up on both sides of the room. Their things were kept in a suitcase beneath the bed. The girls were housed in a second story wing of the convent. Bars were over the windows which were used for safety and to keep anyone from sneaking out. Cele was given a regulation uniform so she blended in with everyone else.

Cele asked the girls lots of questions about the building. She wanted to find out if any doors were left unlocked and if so, when and which ones. Cele was only ten years old at this time and she knew she didn't want any part of the convent and its religion. She bided her time and tried to seek an escape. She found that time one evening when all the nuns went to prayer. She just walked down the stairs and along the hall towards the outside door. She met and saw two women in the linen room as she passed by. She smiled at them and they just smiled back at Cele. She walked outside after spending 7 days in the convent.

Cele walked and ran to some friends home. They were Seven Day Adventists that knew Dad real well. The Kerr family took Cele in. They said a prayer for Cele and gave her dinner and then took her to Kneeland to the Fulton Ranch so Mom couldn't find her. Then they found Dad and told him where Cele was. The Nuns refused to take Cele back when Mom asked them. Mom's lawyer convinced her to drop further proceedings as Dad told her lawyer that Cele would just find a way to escape again.

The main reason, or one reason, that made Cele skeptical about staying with Mom was what she overheard Alice and Mom taking about. Alice was Mom's foster sister. Mom told Alice that she only wanted Cele for baby sitting Cornell. In order for her to get a job and enjoy San Francisco's night life she would need a baby sitter and one that Cornell knew. Another disturbing thing was Cele heard Mom tell Alice that she gave birth to four kids but only claimed one—Cornell.

Cele, Sterl and I were alone much of the time while Dad was on his cattle buying trips. We kept house and looked after the animals. I liked the baby angora goats the best. Occasionally a mother goat would abandon her kid or she might get killed by a cougar or just die. That was when we fed them by bottle. The nipple was 3" long and made from black rubber. It was a good imitation of the mother goats tits. Sometimes the nipple would pop off so I would have milk spill on my dress and shoes so I usually went bare footed. It saved washing shoes. The baby goats got down on their knees when sucking and they like to bunt the bottle as their cute little white tails wagged back and forth. They followed us all around the barn yard bleating for attention. The baby goats had snow white curly hair that was so soft. Along with their soft hair their big blue eyes and pleading cry endeared them to me very much.

On one of my many hiking trips through the forest I found some huge bear tracks in the mud surrounding a small stream. They looked fresh to me so I didn't hang around there long. The tracks would have put "Big Foot" to shame. Talking about Big Foot reminds me of some stories my Uncle Marion Paddock would tell. He was a chopper/faller in the Redwood forest. He and the other woodsmen saw tracks made by some creature other than man and they saw what appeared to be something like a human running through the forest.

Cele's baby was born sometime before the house burned down that winter.

When I was eight years old, Cele was twelve. She grew up fast and her periods started when she was ten years old. She had an experience that was tragic but possibly the result of her early maturity. I wouldn't want this told as long as Cele is alive or it would hurt her to know that I learned about this problem the night it happened. Cele gave birth to a baby boy one night with the assistance of our hired woman and the father of the child. I slept in the next room to Cele's bedroom. The crying out of Cele during the labor woke me up along with the voice of the two people. They tried to be quiet and thought I wouldn't know what was transpiring. I didn't know until I heard a baby cry and then all of a sudden it stopped and didn't cry again. The father who was our 21 year old hired man had choked the baby to death. I heard him telling our housekeeper that he was going to bury it in the woods where no one would find it.

Dad found out what had happened. I think the hired lady told Dad or maybe Sterl found out or knew about the birth and told Dad. I never did know how Dad learned of it.

Dad took Cele and me to Arcata to stay with our friend Dr. Fountain after this happened. He took Cele to our doctor to see if she was okay. While at our friends home Cele and I slept in the double bed in their guest room. One night Dad came to our room to talk with Cele. They thought I was asleep but I was just pretending sleep. He asked Cele if she wanted the hired man arrested for murder or did she want him sent out of the county. I think she was in love with him because she didn't want anything to happen to him like going to jail or getting hanged. Dad had two men friends take him to the San Francisco area and told him never to come back or he would be hung. I overheard Aunt Florence tell Cele this. After this, Dad took Cele and me back to Kneeland to our ranch. Since Cele was always over weight none of us had realized that she was pregnant and she usually wore loose dresses in the summer. I can't remember what month she delivered but it was one of the summer months. After this happened Dad had a school teacher and her husband live with us for a year. The next year he hired another house keeper.

Cele went to school in the fall like nothing had ever happened to her. All of this must have seemed like a bad dream to Cele. I always blamed my mother for this because she had left us to survive on our own knowing that Dad couldn't be home all the time because of his business.

The reason Dad had hired this man to work on our farm was because his family lived quite close to Aunt Flo in Eureka and his mother was single with four children to support. He hit Dad up for a job one day when Dad was visiting Aunt Florence. Dad hired him as a favor to the young man's mother so she would have one less mouth to feed. They lived in an old beat up house that looked like it was ready to fall apart. I think Dad felt sorry for them and this was his way of helping a family in need. Dad was always a compassionate man and lent a helping hand to many people.

Well life for us went on as usual at the ranch except for more and longer visits from Aunt Flo and Grandma and Grandpa Paddock. I don't think that my mother ever knew about Cele's tragic experience but Aunt Florence knew as I heard her talking to Cele about her problem. I guess I always kept my ear tuned into things that were going on.

Aunt Florence's husband, Lee Gregory, used to spend some of his summer vacations with us. He liked to help out with the haying and he was a photographer buff so picture taking consumed a lot of his time. He was a very brilliant man in the engineering field. He was always drawing intricate pictures of some invention that he had in his mind. He was too far advanced in his theories so many people thought he was sort of queer. People during those days were slow to accept new ideas. He was often frustrated and low on patience because no one accepted his ideas.

For the haying season one summer Dad hired a man that was called a half wit to help out. Everyone called him Polly. Dad knew Polly's family quite well and they lived in Freshwater which was on the road to Eureka from our place. On Dad's way home he would stop and pick Polly up so he could work for awhile in order for him to save enough money to buy a car. Polly heard someone say that a certain Ford car could be bought for thirty eight ninety eight. He saved that amount and went to the Ford place and wanted to buy the car for $38.98. When he took out his money and laid it on the counter the store owner just couldn't believe what he saw. The owner and the other employees started laughing and whooping it up. Poor Polly couldn't understand why they wouldn't sell him the car. He got really mad and tore out of the store and ran all the way home which was about five miles. His Dad and other people tried to reason with Polly but he was just too retarded to comprehend such large figures as thousands.

Polly liked my Dad and he trusted Dad so he always tried to do a good job no matter what he was given to do.

One day Lee Gregory was working with Polly pitching hay into our sheep shed. Gregory got mad at Polly because Polly was pitching hay every which way. Soon a screaming argument began and Gregory's anger reached the boiling point. He was so angry he threw the pitch fork at Polly. It hit Polly in the calf of his leg. Polly became so frightened he tore out of the barn yelling that there was a mad man in there. Polly took off running up the road and headed for his home in Freshwater. We couldn't stop him so Sterl ran over to the hay field where Dad was working to tell Dad what happened. Dad came home and got in our Ford pickup and went after Polly. He found him several miles down the road. Blood was still seeping out of the wound so Dad took Polly to his home in Freshwater. Never again did Dad have Gregory and Polly on the ranch at the same time.

I was always trying to fix my hair so it would look pretty but with no one to help me I didn't improve on my looks. Dad usually cut our hair several times a year. We had a curling iron that Cele heated in the hot coals that were in the stove. She would test it on a piece of paper to see how hot it was. She tried curling my hair once but the curling iron slipped and burned my ear so I refused to let her fuss with my hair. Cele managed to put some curl into her hair when she wanted to look pretty.

During my 9th, 10th and 11th years, I spent a great deal of time with Grandma and Grandpa Paddock at their home in Trinidad.

I enjoyed being with Grandpa as he wandered over the land near their home. Many of these walks took us over the railroad trestle which was close to home. We would stop to pick chinkapin nuts that tasted something like hazelnuts but their outer coating was fur-like and stuck to our fingers, hurting us sometimes. Other days he would take a small tin with honey smeared inside as he was interested in finding some honey to harvest from wild bee nests.

I always liked to help and watch Grandma make coffee. She put the green beans in a big pan and baked them in the oven until they were brown. After taking them out of the oven, she would grind the beans in a hand worked grinder. I would turn the handle around and around while Grandma slowly fed the beans into the grinder. Sometimes I was allowed to drink a cup of coffee laced with canned milk and a little sugar. It was quite delicious.

Grandpa's house didn't have an indoor toilet. We used chamber pots at night time and used the outdoor privy during the day. We called them "Chick Sales" or outhouses. My grandparents outhouse had 2 round holes cut into a very wide redwood board. One hole was big and one hole was small. Children used the small hole. For toilet paper we used old Sears Roebuck catalogs or other paper on hand. Old dress patterns were the best. We would wad the catalog pages into a ball and rub them a lot before we used them so they would be softer to use.

When Grandpa and family migrated from South Dakota they brought all of Grandpa's blacksmith tools with them. After they had built their house in Trinidad, Grandpa built a shed for his shop as he still liked to make things and he kept the forge hot most every day even if he was an old man. I loved to watch him use his big bellows to give more life to the coals. Uncle Mary (Marion) and Uncle Billy would help him when they were home. They made hinges, shelf brackets, and many other things.

Thinking back to when I was seven, I remembered a Christmas at Grandpa's house. Uncle Mary, Grandpa, Grandma and I were the only ones there. I felt so alone and wished that Dad would come and get me so I could go to Kneeland and be with Cele and Sterl. Dad had told me that he would come for me before Christmas. So I waited and watched for him and on this Christmas Eve I finally gave up and went to bed. Grandma hadn't planned anything for Christmas as money was very scarce and she didn't think I would be there. Everyone had gone to bed and were sound asleep when Dad did arrive around midnight. He woke me up and gave me a "paper snapper" that someone gave to him to give to me. That was the only present I received that Christmas, just like many others in the past. He brought Grandma a ham and other food stuff which was good because they were short of money and food. Dad always took food and money to give for my keep and to help out. Uncle Mary usually had money to help buy food but he had been out of work for a few months. Grandpa's $40 pension each month didn't always cover all expenses, especially when they had extra mouths to feed.

I will never forget the day a group of Gypsies came driving their canvas covered wagons up the driveway to Grandpa's house. There were three wagons hitched to big horses. Grandma, Lester and I were alone and we were scared. The men stayed in the wagons but a lot of women all dressed in black poured out of the rear openings. They had scarves tied over their heads. They literally started to rush toward us. Grandma quickly told Les and me to go inside and lock all the doors and stay there. These women kept cajoling Grandma and she yelled at them to leave as there was nothing here for them. No money and no food to spare. For a little person who weighed about one hundred pounds and an old lady, she showed them that she had courage. Grandma Paddock kept backing up toward the house until she was at the bottom of the steps leading into the living room. Les and I were watching out the window. All of a sudden Grandma reached into her pocket and pulled out a silver fifty cent piece and handed it to the woman, telling her that this was all the money she had. During the haggling a couple of women walked around the house looking for something to steal. They also asked if they could camp there and Grandma told them that there was a much better place to camp further up the road where there was a lot of grass for the horses to eat. This seemed to placate them and they left.

Grandma's house had 2 bedrooms upstairs and quite a large alcove. I slept in the small bedroom and Lester slept in the alcove as did our cousin Carmen when she stayed with us. My bedroom had dormer windows that looked out toward the road that led to town which was named Trinidad.

Many Indian families lived near us. Some next to our land. Many of the Indian men drank whiskey until they became mean and were prone to fight. Many a night we could hear the "Old Bucks" as they were called, doing their fist fights on the road in front of our house. They reminded me of the bears fighting on Kneeland. There was a lot of grunting, yelling and guttural talk. Les and I would open my windows and listen to them as they fought. It scared us so much as we were afraid they would wander into Grandma's yard. The three of us were alone so that made our fright much worse. One morning Lester and I went down to the place where they fought and we found blood on the ground.

Lester Gregory, Irene Paddock, Cornell Paddock, Lanette Gregory, Carmen Paddock, Claryse Breshears

Since I was the youngest child living at home after Mom left, Dad would leave me with different members of the family when he went on a cattle buying trip. Sometimes I stayed with Aunt Florence, Mabel Poyfaire, a second cousin, or with a neighbor lady, Mal Cosgrove. But most of the time I stayed with Auntie Poyfaire or Grandma. I guess Dad felt that I needed someone other than our housekeeper so when our vacations from school came up he would take me to visit with these people.

I would get less homesick if I stayed with Grandma and Grandpa or Auntie Poyfaire. They always had something going on to keep me busy and interested. Auntie was a great story teller about her life. Auntie Poyfaire, (Charlotte Paddock) was bit by a rattler in her heel when she was eleven years old. This is a story that she loved to tell me since we each shared a rattlesnake story. She was about a mile from her home and going barefoot so she ran as fast as she could to get to her home. Auntie said that she was quite sick for awhile but the place in her heel wasn't a place that was inducive to spread the venom.

Auntie Poyfaire lived until she was 99 years and 10 months old. Her sister Almira Paddock Schofield lived to 103 years. These two girls were Grandpa Paddock's sisters.

Auntie Poyfaire had quite a few books that had fascinating pictures that I always enjoyed.

Auntie's house had electricity, a bath tub, and a flushing toilet so with these luxuries my life was easier. No more padding out to an outhouse at midnight. Another thing that was exciting at Auntie's house was her son Will Poyfaire. He had his own dray business. Will had 3 large Clydesdale horses that he hitched to the dray. Sometimes he would give me a ride and as I sat way, way up on the seat beside him I felt that I owned the world. Will's vocabulary included many cuss words. The horses seemed to understand his vocalizing. The Clydesdales were housed in a barn behind Auntie's house. Being a girl from a mountain ranch, I enjoyed helping Will curry down these huge animals. One of their legs was bigger than me and a hoof as large as my head, but I wasn't afraid because they were very gentle creatures. Will and his team would meet the ships that came into Humboldt Bay and deliver the merchandise to the various stores in Eureka. Did you know that the Clydesdale horses originated in Scotland in the valley of the Clyde river? They were a breed of very strong draft horses, thus so suitable for dray work.

Grandfather passed away on September 26, 1924 at their Trinidad home. He died from the injuries he received when he jumped from the train trestle that he was always walking over. On the day that he fell he was about a third of the way over the trestle when the train came steaming toward him. He turned around and tried to beat the train back to land. He panicked and jumped off the trestle breaking his leg and receiving internal injuries that resulted in his death. The engineer stopped the train about half way over the trestle and yelled to Grandpa to tell him that the train had stopped. Grandpa didn't hear the engineer. Grandma nursed him for three weeks but he never rallied from his injuries.

William Cornell Paddock
Born December 9, 1839
Died September 26, 1924

Attending Grandpa's funeral was my first encounter with death of a loved one. I was 12 years old. I didn't want to believe that he was dead. I asked Aunt Florence if I could kiss Grandfather as he laid in his coffin but she said "I've never seen anyone kiss a dead person". Dad walked with me up to the coffin and as we stood there looking at Grandpa I had a strange feeling that seemed to give me the desire to kiss my dear old Grandpa and so I did. I was surprised to feel the coldness of his body as he looked so natural. I expected him to be warm.

Grandpa was buried with honors by the service of the Ladies of the Grand Army of the Republic because he was a Civil War Veteran. He is buried in the Myrtle Grove cemetery in Eureka, California. Grandma Paddock is buried next to Grandpa Paddock.

I have many fond memories of Grandpa. Especially the times he held me on his knee and sang old army songs. I enjoyed one in particular. "Little Brown Jug". I missed him so much.

Some fun things I did while at Grandma Loena's home when I was younger was making mud pies and decorating them with wild flowers. Grandma put a wide board on a stump of a redwood tree and she gave me lots of metal lids to use for pans. I also played house in the burned out hollowed out stump of a large redwood tree. I made paper dolls and scrapbooks from old magazines. I made paste out of flour and water and boiled it until it was thick for my scrapbook pasting. Grandma always had something to keep me busy. I never had any toys because everyone was too poor to waste money on useless things. Survival was the most important thing.

I wanted to tell you about this before I was 12 years old. I was 10 when I went with Dad to visit an old Indian man and woman who lived near Grandma on the cliff side of some land overlooking the Pacific Ocean. Their shack literally clung to the side of the cliff and was nestled in lots of Alder Trees, Cypress, and wild huckleberries. Pete and Emma were some of the few remaining Indians of their tribe. They were very old. Dad had killed a large buck deer so he brought a hind leg to give to Pete and his wife. In order to get to their cabin we had to walk down a steep, zig-zagging trail. Old Pete had used rocks to make steps where the trail was extra steep.

Loena Roxana (Lasell) Paddock
Born May 28, 1855
Died September 4, 1941

Grandmother's neighbors, the Baker family, had bought the land where Pete and Emma lived from the US Government so Pete and Emma were really squatters. The Bakers let them continue living there.

Pete could speak some English but Emma only spoke Indian. When we visited, she took me aside to show me her little garden, chattering all the time in Indian talk. Of course I just listened and smiled and smiled at her. Such a dear, little old lady with 111 tattooed in blue on her chin. The sign of a married woman. In the meantime Dad was helping Pete hang the deer meat close to his doorway. They talked for quite a spell. Pete was telling Dad about his health which wasn't good. Then he showed us his hand where there were many scars and he had Emma show us her scarred hand. The scars were from "bleeding", which was a practice that their tribe used when they were sick. Dad offered to take them to town to see a doctor, but Pete wouldn't consider that. As we left they both stood at the entrance of their home and watched us go up the trail. Pete had lifted his arm in a farewell salute to us and kept it there as we went beyond their sight. I saw Emma and Pete only once after that. After Pete died, Emma went to live with another Indian family until she died.

We didn't talk much about Mom's abandonment but each of us in our own way missed having a mother. Dad was home as often as possible but buying and selling cattle kept him on the go. Our ranch didn't bring in enough income so Dad earned extra in this way.

One day Dad brought home a crystal set that picked up sound waves from the air. It had a wire attached to a little box and at the tip of the wire there was a plug that we put up to our ear and we could hear music coming through this gadget. To us it was like a toy and we had a lot of fun with it. I remember dad telling us that some day someone would invent a machine that would send out pictures to the world.

Just behind Grandma's house there was a railroad track that ran from Eureka to Trinidad Bay. There was a whaling station at Trinidad so the train hauled the whale oil and all other parts to the ships in Humboldt Bay. Then the ships carried this cargo to San Francisco.

The railroad had a "Cookie Car" that they parked behind Grandma's house. The lady that did the cooking for the crew was an older woman, heavy set and very friendly. When she made doughnuts and cookies she would call to Lester and me to come and get a treat. She often gave us some other left over foods like roast beef. She liked to visit with us and asked us to bring Grandma to visit. We were happy for her friendship as it added some spice to our secluded lives.

Grandma never turned a hobo (tramp) away if he offered to chop some wood in exchange for food. Living next to the railroad spur seemed to bring more of the tramps as they rode the rails looking for some kind of work. They never caused us any harm and they were so thankful for the food. Grandma was happy to get the wood split. We always gave them a loaf of home made bread and whatever else Grandma had cooked. Sometimes a jar of beans or stew was a treat for the men and I will always remember the time she gave the hobo half of a pumpkin pie. That man's face lit up like a lighted Christmas tree.

The train would stay parked for a day or two depending on when a whaling ship would come into the bay with a whale. The foreman would blow a whistle when one came in that could be heard at least five miles away to inform people that a whale had arrived. On one of these days Uncle Marion took Lester and me up to see the huge whale. It turned out to be one of the largest ever brought into the station. The whale was on the platform being prepared for butchering when we arrived. The men had it's mouth braced open with 4x6 posts. The workers let people step inside the mouth just to see how big it was. The men could stand upright and never touch the top of the whale's mouth. Lester and I were helped into the mouth and stood there so very carefully. Les was clutching my hand and we were both frightened. Les was only about 4 years old at this time. I was 11, (almost 12). That whale was over 80 feet long. Grandma thought it was terrible that all these whales were being killed. When the whaling whistle would blow she would say "There goes another poor creature to the knives of men".

The summer when I was staying with Grandma, two of the men stationed on the railroad gave Lester a very bad scare. He was about 7 years old. The men would call him to come and see them while they offered him some goodie or on this occasion they lured him up to where they sat on a redwood log by offering him a jack knife. When he got there one man had his pants down showing his penis. He tried to get Lester to feel him. Lester was so confused he just stood there until the other man laughed and grabbed Lester by his arm and tried to drag him up to the exposed man. I was outside and heard Les yelling for us. I ran up there and when they saw me they laughed and tried to coax me up to where they were. I turned around and ran back to get Grandma. This scared the men enough to let go of Les and he ran lickety-split to the house. Grandma told the "Cookie" lady about this and we weren't allowed to go there when the men were eating their meals. The men came in for their lunch and dinner and slept in the bunk cars. Lester and I were afraid of them so we steered clear of the outfit. In those days we never heard of a pedofile or homosexual. Lester and I talked to Grandma about this as we just couldn't understand why those 2 men pulled their pants down and exposed themselves as we had been taught to keep our clothes over our bodies.

I think I was about 10 years old when I sat down in a nest of bees while I was out in the woods back of Grandma's house. I was stripping bark from the Cascara Trees so I could sell it. Since I had been out there all morning, I had to go to the toilet so I selected a dense thicket where I could hide and I didn't see any bees nest in the ground. I had about 30 stings on my bottom. Grandma pulled the stingers out and put some Lysol salve on my bottom. It was very uncomfortable to sit for a few days.

Dad took me to a baseball game in Eureka when I was 11. That was a most exciting day as Dad bought me a bag of peanuts and a hot dog. It was my first hot dog and it was so very delicious with the mustard oozing on the bun. Of course I didn't know much about the game but enjoyed watching the players hit the ball. We played baseball in school but not like this. Most of the audience was made up of men and boys. I didn't mind this at all. Just the excitement of the crowd, their cheering and yelling and I was with my Dad. That was enough for me. That was a very special day for me. I will always remember the hats that most of the men wore. A sea of fedora hats with their wide brims—some gray, black and a few brown ones. Hats, hats, hats everywhere. A sea of hats.

Dad also took me to town with him when I was 11. We rode in the "Tin Lizzy" which was fun. When we got to Eureka the Ringling Brothers Circus was in town so Dad took me to see my first circus. Another first for me was a large cone shaped strawberry ice cream cone. I was so delighted and happy to be receiving these special treats. As I write this I can almost taste that delicious ice cream. Up until this, all we ever had was home made vanilla ice cream which was made during the winter when we could gather the big icicles that hung from the house and barns. We sure enjoyed licking the paddles after the ice cream was frozen. Sometimes when the snow was frozen we would put sugar in some very thick cream and mix it with the frozen snow. This was a treat for us. In those days there weren't any pollutants to get in the snow and we never had any stomach aches from eating snow or icicles.

One day during the hot summer time Dad drove home a little Ford Pickup to be used on the farm. I told Dad that I wanted to learn how to drive so he said, "Fine, I'll teach you". We took jaunts to visit the neighbors and used it to spotlight deer and rabbits. Bill James was courting Cele so he learned how to drive when he came to visit us. He drove when we went spotlighting. Sterl was also learning how to drive. I thought that I had learned how to drive just by watching Dad so one day I got it started and drove it across the front of our yard and ended up hitting an Oak tree which stalled the pickup. I didn't know how to stop it as I hadn't learned where the brake was located. After this episode Dad gave me some driving lessons. Reminds me of the time, Gayle, when your Dad made you drive up the highway in our station wagon to help drive our cattle back home. You were 11 too and you had never driven before.

When Sterl was 11 years old he had a female bear try to attack him. She had 2 cubs and was protecting them. Sterl was out hunting for a deer when he surprised the mother. She came down the path at a run for Sterl. He had his 300 Savage rifle and shot her. She dropped dead about 5 feet from Sterl. When dad came home he took Sterl and the hired man to bring the bear carcass home and to try and catch the baby cubs. They caught one but couldn't find the other one. Dad sent the cub to San Francisco to the zoo and sold the bear carcass to the Chinese people in San Francisco.

One of Old Bill Poyfaire's Clydesdale horses kicked Sterl in the head when Sterl was 14 years old. The horse was very old and stoved up so he was put out to pasture on our ranch as he wasn't fit to pull a dray anymore. Old Bill didn't want to kill his horse so since he had to be put out to pasture we took him. The horse got along quite well during the hot summer months but when the days turned cold in the fall, he would get so stiff that Sterl and Bill James had a hard time getting him up on his feet. When Dad saw how difficult it was to take care of the horse he got permission to shoot it from Old Bill Poyfaire. On the day it kicked Sterl, the horse had been pulled to its feet with much slapping, yelling and pulling. It was trembling and wobbly on its huge feet. Sterl got his 300 Savage rifle and was carrying it as he walked behind the horse. Bill James was leading it because they didn't want to shoot it near the house. The horse was having a very difficult time walking so Sterl thought it might help it he twisted its tail like they did with the cows. I guess Sterl wanted to hurry things up a bit and they didn't have much further to go before shooting the animal. All of a sudden as Sterl was twisting its tail it lifted his huge foot and kicked back hitting Sterl in the forehead. Sterl was knocked out cold and didn't regain consciousness for a long time. Dad wasn't home and we didn't have a car so he couldn't take Sterl to see a doctor. Bill carried him into the house and laid him on the bed. Cele wiped Sterl's face to clean the blood and dirt off. Other than that we didn't know what to do. Dad got home late that night so the next morning he took Sterl to town to see Dr. Curtis Falk, our family doctor.

Sterling F. Paddock

Sterl was finishing up his 8th grade at school and the term was going to end shortly. Graduation plans were all made but Sterl couldn't go because of his injury. The school term was extended because of the previous bad winter. Sterl wasn't there for the final tests so he didn't get his diploma and never went back to complete his work. It took Sterl a long time to feel well again.

Sterl said that he felt like something was dripping in his head. He was injured just above his eyes along his forehead. The doctor said Sterl was lucky as a kick in that part of the head could have lifted the top of his head off.

Dad took Sterl and me to San Francisco soon after Sterl's accident. Dad's friend drove us down and we returned by train. We visited with Mom. It was the first time that we saw her and Cornell after she left Eureka. She lived in an apartment on a hill above the city and rode a cable car to her place of employment. She was a telephone operator. Cornell was 10 years old, Sterl 14, and I was 12 so it was like getting acquainted for the first time. I spent 2 days with Cornell and Mom. Sterl and dad rented a hotel room.

I will always remember Mom making toast for me in a relatively new gadget—an electric toaster. It kept burning the toast so she ended up browning the bread in a fry pan.

On this trip to San Francisco, we stopped at Luther Burbanks's place. Dad was interested in grafting and fruit culture. Dad told us that Burbank would be famous some day as he had crossed the orange and lemon to produce a new fruit. Turned out to be the grapefruit.

Mr. Burbank was a very friendly man and was happy to tell Dad all about his work. We stayed there about an hour. As we were leaving, Mr. Burbank gave us some oranges to take on our journey to San Francisco. Dad was going down to San Francisco to see a heart doctor.

When we got there we rented a basement apartment for 2 weeks.

Cele and Bill were married the following February. They moved into the little 3 room cabin that was just below the main residence. Since Cele and Bill were planning on getting married Dad hired Bill to work for us. Bill had been courting Cele for some time, coming over from the Rousseau ranch most weekends. He rode his horse and as he approached our ranch he would blow his coronet to alert Cele of his arrival.

Of course he was serenading Cele. Cele and Bill were married in Trinidad. A local preacher came to perform the ceremony on the 1st of February, 1926.

One chore I hated to do was squeeze grubs out of the milk cows backs. The horse fly laid its eggs just beneath the skin. Sterl helped and taught me how to bind the grubs. We slid our hand down their back and when we felt a lump we knew we had found a grub. Sterl was good at getting them out. It wasn't very easy for me but with my minuscule help, we kept the grubs at bay. Dad gave us a bucket filled with some kind of disinfectant that we poured over their backs. This helped to heal the wounds and sure did make the cows feel better.

When I was 13 I got my drivers license. Dad took me to an office down town and they didn't give me a test of any kind. They just asked my age, eye color, height and weight and presto, I had a license. It was revoked when I was 29 years old. I was married and Gayle was a baby, 9 months old. We were living in Half Moon Bay, California so I had to drive to Redwood City to renew my license. Of course I took baby Gayle along so she was with me and I didn't have to take any tests. They just issued me a new card.

Since my Dad had several light strokes, his health wasn't good so he was programming me to become his chauffeur. This was a good thing because one night after dark, Dad and I were driving home to our Kneeland ranch and the fog was like pea soup. All of a sudden Dad stopped the car by the side of the road and told me he was too sick to drive and I would have to take over and get us home. After I got in the drivers seat I put the Model T in low gear and left it there as I drove up the steep, winding gravel road. As I drove in this thick fog through the towering redwood trees along the sides of the road I was so scared all the way home and my 13 year old body was tied up in lots of knots. I will never forget how hard I gripped that steering wheel. My hands felt numb from the pressure and it took us about 2 hours to make the trip home. This was my first driving trip with no help from Dad as he had closed his eyes and rested his head on the back of the seat all the way home. After this night I did almost all of the driving for Dad until he passed away when I was 16. He was 46.

My first boyfriend was 14 years old. We sat next to each other in school and shared a double desk. His Dad was the government hunter to track down cougars or panthers that were killing ranchers sheep and calves. They also took care of the coyote problem and occasionally a bear. We had lots of all these animals on our ranch. Dad would call the hunter when a panther would scream and get close to our place at night. As I said earlier, they brought their dogs, lanterns and other equipment and stayed at our house. We fed them and bedded them down. Sometimes it took several days to track down a marauding animal. They often hunted at night as that is when some animals prowl.

The son of this man went to our school. His name was Charles Millsap. His family had moved to Kneeland and lived there for a year until the wild animals were under control. I was in the 7th grade and he was in the 8th grade. He had black hair and gray eyes and to me he was very handsome. His manners were much better than most of the hillbilly boys. He was a great teaser and liked to wink at me. He was my first love. I was so sad when they moved to another area. He said he would try and come back for a visit which he never did because a few months after they moved into a new place he caught diphtheria and died. He called me Renee and asked his Dad to let me know that he was sick. Needless to say I had a broken heart for a long time.

I was 15 when Dad bought a new Chevrolet Coach Car for 700 dollars. It was painted two toned green and it had a Fisher body, box like in shape. I was very proud to drive our new car and enjoyed all our trips. One in particular was a trip to Portland, Oregon. We took Lester Gregory and Grandma Paddock to visit Grandma's sister, Aunt Bertha Lasell Osborne and her 2 children. This was the last long trip that Dad took and my first trip to a large city. I was still 15 then. We had a few close calls on our way and to this day Lester Gregory accuses me of driving like a demon. I got on a one way street in Portland, going the wrong way. There wasn't much traffic as it was very early in the morning but a milk delivery truck was driving towards us and the driver just kept on coming straight at me. I pulled over and he stopped to inform me that I should turn around and go the other way. He was very kind and helpful by giving us directions to Aunt Bertha's home. Another booboo was when we came upon a highway construction with lots of small detours. One was so poorly marked that we couldn't figure out which way to go. I took the right side and ended up on the new cement road. I thought this was great because it felt so smooth driving. Then we came upon a group of construction workers who were shouting and waving their hands at us. I continued on at a slow speed until a man who came running toward us stopped us. He told me to turn around fast and get out of there or I'd be fined a lot of money if the foreman saw me. Thank goodness the cement was hard enough to prevent damage to the new road.

Dad, Grandma, and Lester put their complete faith in my driving. Today as I think about that trip to Portland, it is a miracle that we came out safe. I did take a few hair raising maneuvers while passing some cars.

One car that I was following for a long time gave me much concern. The road was a very curvy winding road thru a forest of huge cedar trees. He would slow down and move over into the middle of the road. Night was coming on and it was becoming quite dark. I didn't like the situation as I felt threatened and scared. Soon we came to a wide place where I could drive off the road and get past the car so gunned the motor and sped past this car so fast I hardly realized what I was doing. I kept up the speed for awhile even if the curves were a problem as I wanted to get away from this threat. They speeded up and followed us until we arrived at a small settlement that had a gas station and some cabins to rent. We stayed there that night. The car that caused me so much anxiety also stopped. Two men, rough looking characters, got out and wanted to rent a cabin but the owner was filled up as we had taken his last rental. The owner told Dad that they looked like a couple of rough characters and was glad he couldn't accommodate them.

The Paddocks
L-R: Sterling F. Paddock, Lucille R. Paddock, Garfield Lincoln Paddock, Irene F. Paddock, and William C. "Nelly" Paddock

On this trip I was so embarrassed when we had our luggage inspected at the California/ Oregon border. Cele had given me a pair of pea-green under panties for my birthday. They were silk and so beautiful. All my under clothes were cotton so I really felt very feminine and special with Cele's gift. It was the only gift I received for my birthday and I know that Cele had to save her pennies in order to buy me a gift. I took them on my trip. Two men at the border were looking for fresh fruit that was not allowed to be transported from one state to another. They lifted up my underwear etc. and that was something that shocked me. They seemed to enjoy our embarrassment and it certainly wasn't necessary to hold up teddy bear underwear.

All of us enjoyed our visit with Aunt Bertha Osborne and her family of 2, Hubert and Roxana. Grandma Paddock was so happy to visit with her sister as it had been years since they saw each other.

Dad and I left Grandma's house on our arrival home to go back to Kneeland where we took up our usual duties of ranch life. The weather was quite a change from Trinidad. It sure was hot but we suffered through it. Except for Dad. He spent one night at home and headed for Eureka the next morning. He couldn't take the heat and higher altitude because of his heart problem. This was the last trip that Dad took. I spent my 16th birthday at Kneeland. I stayed at home to help out with the chores. Since Cele and Bill were married I took over the household for Sterl and Dad. I also separated the cream from the milk so we could haul it in 5 gallon milk cans to the creamery in Arcata. Sterling did most of the chores concerning the animals. He milked about 12 cows by himself. To survive we needed the money from the sale of cream so Sterl milked and I separated the cream. We had a little milk house just below the main house. Separators had lots of little plates fitted together and when we turned the crank the milk flooded thru the plates and bingo, we had thick rich cream. Washing all those plates was the hard part. We saved the evening milk and mixed it with the morning milk so I had to wash them up just once a day. We took the cream to town once or twice a week. The creamery tested each batch. If it was a little bit sour that was okay but if it had a bad or spoiled smell they wouldn't take it. So during the hot summer we took it more often to the creamery. When we couldn't get to town we would send it on the stage. Many of the ranchers on Kneeland depended on this source of income to buy their staple foods.

The year that I was approaching my 15th birthday was spent by going on many trips around the county with Dad. On a day that we were headed for home Dad brought up the subject of sex and men. I was surprised as he had never talked to me about his sensitive subject. He said, "Renee, I'm expecting a man to stop by the ranch sometime soon and I want to warn you about his character. He has been known to seduce young girls. Dad also warned Cele about this man and told Sterl to keep a close watch on him. He did stop at our house on his way to Eureka. We gave him his dinner and let him sleep in the barn. Since our house had burned down and was only replaced with a 4 room house we couldn't offer him sleeping quarters. I wondered why Dad had warned me about this man. He looked harmless to me. He gave us no trouble and left the next morning after a good breakfast of pancakes and deer steak. Years later I learned that he had molested and raped his own daughter. Cele told me about it years later after we had moved to Othello

I helped Grandma with many chores such as cleaning house, doing the dishes and hauling water to her garden plants. She treasured many of her plants—especially the star jasmine. She had plants that she had brought with her from South Dakota. One of her rose bushes is still growing at the old house where Lester now lives. All the other plants are gone.

Most of my 15th year was spent at Kneeland as I was trying to help Dad. I often had to do the driving for him as he traveled around our county doing business. Up to this time Dad had about 5 heart attacks and he dragged one leg all the time. He didn't feel secure in his driving so much.

I had my 16th birthday while living at our Kneeland home. My neighbors son liked to tease me a lot by singing this ditty to me. "My Irene, sweet sixteen, the village queen." I hated it because I didn't like the young man. He was 20 years old and to me was too old to be carrying on like this. I never celebrated my birthdays, not cakes, no gifts, no parties. Birthdays just meant that I was getting older and was acquiring a more mature attitude. None of us celebrated birthdays.

July 1, 1928 was a very warm and you could say a hot day. Sterl and I were alone most of the day. Dad arrived from Eureka that evening and he said,

"Renee, you're 16 now, a fine young lady and I am glad to have all your help to me. I would like to do more for you and Sterl." We had a good family talk and Dad asked Sterl and me what idea we might have in regard to our future. Sterl wanted to farm, and I wanted to go to high school in Eureka so I could be prepared to study nursing, which was my first wish. My second wish was to be a teacher. It really wasn't much difference but nursing seemed to be my favorite. Well, dad said that for the time it wouldn't be possible for me to go to school. Aunt Florence offered to let me stay with her and Lynette and I could go to school together, but this idea was postponed. Dad needed me at home so I spent most of the summer keeping house for Sterl and Dad.

Several months before Dad died he bought me a beautiful little horse, a filly, and a racing cart. Her name was Phyllis and she was very gentle and a loving creature who enjoyed being with people. She would whinny every time I went to feed her. Dad thought I needed some kind of transportation so I could visit our neighbors that lived 2 or 3 miles from us and also to collect the mail from the post office. Sterl would help me hitch her to the cart and away up the road I would go. Such fun, and I felt a sense of freedom as I had never felt before.

Dad told me that I could race her at the Eureka tracks after I became used to her. This I never had an opportunity to do as Dad passed away the following November. I only had her from spring time to fall. She was sold and the money turned into the estate fund.

Dad wasn't feeling well all summer. Around the later part of October 1928 Dad had stayed home much of the time. One night he came home rather late as he had a neighbor drive for him. The son drove Dad's car and the father followed in their car. This was November 2, 1928. Dad always brought fresh food from Eureka each time he came home. This was around 10:00 o'clock. He had brought some salmon steaks so I cooked them and fixed some hash brown potatoes. He seemed to enjoy his meal as salmon was always one of his favorite foods. After he ate his dinner he visited with Sterl and me. He didn't feel well. Then Dad went to bed which was earlier than he usually retired. Around midnight he woke Sterl and me and said, "I'm so sick, can you help me get dressed and take me to town." We needed help so I ran down

DIED

PADDOCK—Garfield L. Paddock, died at Eureka, November 3, 1928, about 7:00 p. m. He has for the past ten years been a resident of Kneeland Prairie Section. He was born June 25, 1882, and leaves his mother, Mrs. Leona Paddock, of Trinidad; four children: Mrs. Vancell James, Irene, Sterling and Cornell Paddock of Kneeland; three brothers, Marion and William D. Paddock, of Trinidad, and George Paddock of Orick; one sister, Mrs. Guy Breshears, of Eureka; and an aunt, Mrs. Charlotte Poyfaire of Eureka.

The funeral will be from Pierce Funeral Parlors in Eureka, Wednesday, at 1:30 P. M. Friends and acquaintances are invited. 11-4-1

Obituary of Garfield Lincoln Paddock

to the cabin where Cele and Bill lived and got them up to help. Dad was having a stroke so couldn't talk too well. We got him in the car and took him to Eureka to the hospital. We stayed at the hospital for a long time. Then the nurses sent Cele and me home with Aunt Florence. Dad lingered on until the next day, November 3, 1928. He died in the early morning. Sterl and Bill had sat up with him until he passed away. They then came home and we knew Dad was dead. We buried Dad at Sunset Memorial Cemetery. His funeral was very large as he knew so many people. Someone said they had never seen such a large procession of people at any funeral in Eureka.

We rented the ranch to Tim Berry. Cornell and I were minors so we each received $20 a month for our support. Cornell moved back to San Francisco to live with Mom. Sterl was 18 so he didn't need a guardian. Sterl went to live with Luther Sibley and remained working with him until Luther died. Uncle Billy was our guardian. Billy sold off all the livestock.

Uncle Billy had Aunt Florence keep the books for all the money from the sale of equipment and live stock. I never did know how much money was collected. It paid for Dad's funeral and some outstanding bills like the taxes. Uncle Billy was gone so much of the time that he put Aunt Florence in charge of things. She was paid for her work.

Aunt Florence sold the new house that Dad had built. She kept most of the money but gave Cele, Sterl, and me $200 from the sale. It was sold for $2,900. I asked Aunt Florence what happened to the rest of the money. She said Dad owed it to her husband, Guy Bresheres. Dad did owe him $350 as I kept Dad's books. I knew she lied to me. Cele & Sterl wouldn't stand up to Aunt Florence so I did and so I was the black sheep in the family. Cele was married to Bill and they moved to Eureka where Bill got a job working for a slaughter house. The owner, Fred Wolloper, had been a good friend of Dads.

I lived for awhile with Aunt Florence. Then I moved to Trinidad and lived with Grandma. While living with Grandma, I went to Arcata High School and graduated from there. I lived with Grandma all during my high school education. Lester and Uncle Marion stayed with her also. Lester was in grade school. Uncle Marion worked at odd jobs and was gone much of the time. Uncle Billy was a carpenter so lived in various places. He built a lot of barns in the Kneeland area. He had asthma so when he got sick he would come home to Grandma's.

Uncle Marion would take Lester and me down to Luffin Holes which was on the beach about 3 miles from home when I was living with Grandma at Trinidad. Uncle Mary was a good mechanic so he kept his old car in good shape, thus we would pile into his car with all our clamming gear such as shovel, pails, and boots and head for some fun. Good clamming depended on the ocean tides. Sometimes we had to get up very early so before leaving the house we would get several slices of Grandma's home made bread and freshly churned butter to eat as we rode in the old dilapidated car. Clamming was always so much fun. As the tide receded we would search for the clam's water spouts, like a small bubble on the smooth surface of sand. These Razor Back Clams were very large. Many of them were at least 12 inches long. On good days it didn't take us long to get our limit. When we got home we cleaned them, first working off the sand, then using a pocket knife we opened their shells and cut out the insides. We separated the tougher parts to be used in soup, and fried the tender parts. Delicious. After Mom and Cornell came home from San Francisco, Cornell was 18 and could drive. He would pick Lester and me up to go clamming with him. Mom made delicious clam fritters for us.

My summers were spent on Kneeland at the Sibley ranch. I worked for Mr. Sibley by doing the cooking for his hired help and thrashing crew. Thank goodness by this time I had learned how to make gravy which was always appreciated by the men. Gravy could make anything taste good.

One day all I had to cook was liver which I knew the men didn't like, so I got out the old hand grinder and ground the liver with some onions. I drained the juice off, added a little flour and fried it in bacon drippings. I had liver patties which went over big with the men. The gravy helped. Since living so far from town we couldn't run out to the grocery store to get something for dinner. I cooked a lot of potatoes and beans and Sterl almost always had fresh meat for me to cook. The deer were plentiful on Kneeland and easy to hunt. When the weather was hot we couldn't keep the meat very long so Sterl made jerky out of the parts I didn't use. I'd cook up a few roasts and make venison stew which kept well for several days.

Mr. Sibley never paid me and one summer Uncle Marion worked for him so he gave us a milk cow which we took to Grandma's place. That was our pay. I didn't enjoy being there but I had room and board for my work. One summer Lynette spent about a month with me so it wasn't so lonely. Henri Rousseau would ride his horse when he came to visit us. Lynette had a crush on him. Henri also like to visit with Uncle Sterl. Then Lynette finished high school and college and Henri returned from World War II. He married Lynette in August, 1945.

During this time of my life I didn't have many young friends because we were so isolated and I spent much of my time going with Dad on his cattle buying trips. Sometimes I stayed with Aunt Florence.

Aunt Florence had a neighbor lady who had 3 daughters. One was my age so she invited me to stay overnight with her. We slept in a double bed that was in a lean-to on the back of their house. She told me that she had a boy friend who would climb in the window at night and sleep with her. She said that if he came that night I could have him. This frightened me so much that I stayed awake most of the night. He didn't show up that night. I told Aunt Florence about it and that was the last time I stayed with her.

I was 15 and getting educated to things that I had never heard of. While I was with Aunt Florence I also had met another neighbor and her family. The mother was a Swedish lady from the old country and had 6 daughters. She was very friendly and a great talker with a broken accent. Her younger daughter liked to visit with Lynette and me as we were about the same age. During this time while staying with Aunt Florence I enrolled at a private business college in Eureka. Aunt Cele was also attending this school. The neighbor's daughter was going to this school so the mother talked Aunt Florence into sending Cele and me. This took place soon after Dad had died. While attending this school several of the girls and I were including the neighbor's daughter in our activities. We planned a day at the beach so took a ferry from Eureka to Samoa. All 6 of us contributed food for a picnic lunch.

We spent our time looking for shells, agates, and other flotsam and just laying around on the sand enjoying the sunshine. We played games, had water fights and went bare footed into the waves. I don't remember this family's name. On this day, her daughter gave all of us a type written paper all nicely folded and asked us to keep it until we got home to read its contents which we did. I put my copy in my coat pocket because I didn't have a purse.

As the sun was getting low in the sky we gathered our things and headed for the ferry and home. All of us were quite exhausted and ready to go. During our walk to the ferry, the daughter kept putting her arms around several of the girls and hugging them. After we got off the ferry I took a street car home to Aunt Florence's. As I rode home I took the folded letter out of my pocket and read it. The daughter had written each of us a love letter and described things that she could do to us to make us happy. I didn't understand half of what she wrote so I folded it up and put it back in my pocket. When I got home I took the letter out and was unfolding it to show it to Lynette and Aunt Florence. Before I could show it to Lynette, Aunt Florence snatched it out of my hands, read it and kept it. When she saw the girls name at the bottom of the letter, I think Aunt Florence knew the girl was a lesbian. That was the end of that relationship and we tried to avoid the girl while in school as Aunt Florence suggested.

I was getting educated fast after Dad died and living in a city for the first time. When the term at the business school ended I got a job working at Woolworth which was a dime store in the jewelry section. I was still 16 and green as green could be.

During this time I stayed sometimes with Auntie Charlotte Poyfaire, sometimes with Cele and Bill or Aunt Florence, Mabel Poyfaire, and Grandma Paddock. It wasn't a chore to move from one place to another as what little I had I could carry in a couple of paper bags. I didn't have a suitcase.

After the Christmas holidays, I stayed with Cele. They were living in one of Pappy James houses in Eureka. Cele had contacted a light case of tubercular lung disease. She had a few lesions on her lungs so the doctor put her to bed. I took care of her. Everything had to be sterilized so I used Lysol in the water for washing clothes and dishes. It smelled awful and burned my hands as I was using it too strong.

This was during the Great Depression. We had plenty to eat as Bill raised chickens, had a milk cow and a vegetable garden. He also had a job working for the State of California on the county roads. He earned $28 a month. Bill earned too much to get any food supplements like flour and sugar. I was getting $20 a month from Dad's estate so Aunt Florence and Cele were pleased to give me a home so I turned my money over to them.

I remember helping Cele sew up chicken crops because the hens had gorged themselves on grain and then they became crop bound. They would have died if left alone. We would part the feathers and pull a few out in a straight line on the crop so a cut could be made about 2 to 3 inches long. The swollen grain would almost pour out of them. Then Cele sewed the cut up with plain white thread and then put the chicken in a quiet place to recover for a couple of days.

I didn't have any furniture at Cele's so I slept on the floor in their bedroom with a couple of hand made quilts for a mattress.

When living with Cele, she and I had our first permanents. The beauty operators used electric rollers to create steam when applied to wet hair. This was an experimental procedure. The steam burned my scalp in some places where the protective padding was too thin. We volunteered to have a demonstration permanent so it was free. The heat from the steam curled the hair as they didn't have any chemicals to use. I had a soft, wavy curl which only lasted for about a month.

When my dime store job ended after Christmas and Cele had recovered, I went back to live with Grandma Paddock. About a year later I took side trips to stay with Auntie Poyfaire or Aunt Florence.

Uncle Billy and Uncle Marion never did get married. It was rumored around Trinidad that Uncle Marion had a part Indian girl friend. She must have fathered his child because the gossips said that she had a red headed child and Uncle Marion had curly red hair. Aunt Florence also had red hair.

When Uncle Marion came home from visiting his girl friend which was usually around midnight he was very drunk so with his stumbling around and making a lot of noise as he tried to find his bed in the dark, he always woke all three of us up. Grandma got up to administer to him. Since we didn't have electricity for light, she lit several coal oil lamps as she couldn't trust him with the lamps. After she got him to bed and quieted down, she stayed up for awhile to make sure that everything was fine. Usually it wasn't. He usually got sick to his stomach after consuming the rot-gut wine that the Indians made. Next morning, Grandma always made excuses for Uncle Mary by saying "That poor boy is so sick. I guess he ate some bad food or he's getting the flu". Of course Les and I knew what made him sick but we never let Grandma know that we had heard by the grape vine that it was some Indian's "rot-gut".

Sterl had some money to buy his clothes and personal items. I earned spending money by baby sitting our neighbors grand daughter and picking berries when they were in season while living at Trinidad.

While attending high school I rode the bus from Trinidad to Arcata. I used to walk thru the redwoods on our neighbors land to catch the bus.

My neighbors, the Bakers, had raised a fawn who when it was fully grown and getting antlers became mean. One day on my way home from school it took after me and I ran behind a tree. I picked up some sticks and threw them at the deer which distracted him for awhile so I could dart behind another tree further away where there was more undergrowth. I remained real quiet. Then the buck turned away and headed for the neighbors house. Uncle Marion told them that the deer was dangerous and that it had chased me through the woods. I sure got home fast when I thought I could be safe to run. The Bakers decided that the deer might be a problem and put him down. They used the meat so it wasn't a total bad ending.

I was about 18 years old when I started high school. About the same age as the seniors but there were quite a few students like me. Getting a late start wasn't unusual. Some of the teachers, fresh out of college, weren't much older that I.

My art teacher and P.E. teacher took me and another girl out on the golf course to give us an opportunity to learn how to play. It was fun but we didn't have the money to keep it up. I tried out for every sport that was offered to girls and always made the team. You name it and I did it. I liked badminton, tennis, and soccer the best. We didn't have swimming as we didn't have a pool. Most of the kids learned how to swim in small streams that were dammed up by using gunny sacks filled with dirt. We had done this to the stream that ran through our ranch so Cele, Sterl and I learned how to swim—frog fashion. I learned how to float by just laying still in the water with my arms along my sides.

We didn't mind the long walk down as we anticipated the cooling effects of the crystal clear water. The climb back out of the canyon was fine since the sun was beginning to go down and the tall trees shaded us as we climbed.

I enjoyed my high school years and anticipated the benefits I would acquire each day. I had to work hard to catch up with most of the students because of my sketchy grade school classes. I entered into most of the activities offered including sports, and various clubs. Even debating. I made friends with many of the students even if they weren't in my class.

I had so few clothes to wear so it was hard to keep them fresh, and clean. No electric irons, just old, heavy, sad irons. Seemed like Lester and I were always washing out an outfit at night and pressing it out the next morning. Lester did his own things and I did mine. We had a plunger that worked like a toilet plunge. It was made of wood and (or metal) with 5 foot long handle. We filled the galvanized tub half full with warm or hot water, added soap, then the clothes. With much beating up and down we got most of the dirt out. Of course we had to heat the water on Grandma's wood burning stove. We wore the old wooden plunger out so Uncle Mary made us a metal one. He worked scraps of worn out buckets for the paddles and cranked up Grandpa's blacksmith shop to form the metal. When I was little, and Grandpa was well enough to fire up the furnace, I would stand just inside the shop and watch him hammer pieces of ret hot metal as he fashioned some tool or repaired some things. The sparks flew, water sizzled, and loud resounding noises were fascinating to me.

The old shop stood still after Grandpa died. I was 12 and I sure did miss that kind, white whiskered, old man. The shop is used for a woodshed today, the old bellows gone, the smell still seems to linger on.

Uncle Billy helped build the Trinidad house for Grandma and Grandpa Paddock. He also helped to build their C Street home in Eureka. Grandpa had all 3 of his sons helping him with the building. They were young men and very helpful in getting their parents established.

The old redwood sink was still in use when I lived with Grandma. There was a faucet for cold water which was piped in from a spring. When I was living there I used a lye solution to scrub and wash the sink. I also scrubbed the redwood plank floor in the kitchen with the lye solution. It left the redwood a bright rosy pink color and it sure looked clean and pretty for quite a few days.

Cele and Bill inherited the family car so they would drive me to Trinidad to stay with Grandma. Uncle Billy or Uncle Marion would drive me to Kneeland to spend the summer at the Sibley ranch. This was about the only time I got to see Sterl as he rarely came to visit anyone in town.

The only way I had to earn money during this time of my life was picking wild berries and baby sitting for my neighbors grand child and spending the summers at the Sibley ranch where I didn't get any money—only board and room. I also received a small sum each year from the rent on our ranch. Uncle Billy handled this and I never knew how much money was paid to us. I used my share for college tuition which was $70 for half a year.

When Cornell was 18 years old he and Mom returned to Humboldt County from San Francisco. They moved into the 4 room house on the Paddock ranch. This house was built by Uncle Billy and it replaced the one that had burned down. It was a rough, bare boards and no amenities house, more like a cabin than a house.

Cornell raised a few calves and he worked at a lumber mill in Eureka. Mom also worked for a lady in Eureka doing house work. Cornell had an old car so he drove Mom and himself to town every day.

Kitty, the lady Mom worked for asked Mom to move into her house and take care of it as Kitty had a home in San Francisco and preferred living there. She only used this house for vacations and visiting relatives.

Mom worked there for a long time. Cornell remained at Kneeland. He also worked for a rancher on Kneeland, Tim Mullen. That is where he met Frances. She was Tim's niece.

During this time I was attending college at Humboldt State University. I lived with the Brizard family and earned my board and room plus $5 a month by cleaning, washing clothes, and cooking and other household chores.

Summers I worked for the Lebembaums who owned the Eureka Inn and a summer resort at Redwood Groves. I helped with the cooking, dish washing, and cleaning their cabin. The Lebembaums entertained their San Francisco friends there. They treated me like one of their family and even included me in their card games, teaching me how to play Mahjong, Cribbage, and other games. I loved it there. The towering redwood trees were huge and the Eel River ran through their camp. We went swimming every day. Mrs. Lebembaum was pregnant so she brought her maid, a young girl like me, to spent the summer with us. Life was exciting for me as everything was so new for me and I had a young friend to share my free time with. At this summer camp were some of the best years of my young life. When summer was over I stayed with the Brizard family in Arcata where I attended college.

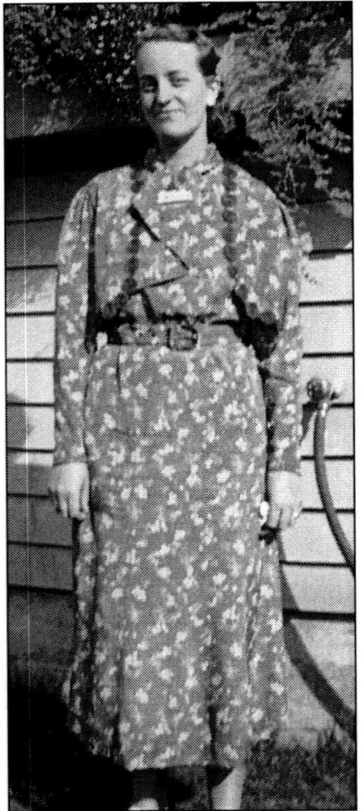

Irene Florence (Paddock) Ivory—taken about 1932

Mrs. Lebembaum came from Lebanon. Her father sent her here to save her life as the Jewish people were being killed and slaughtered as fast as they could be found. Her father was a doctor but he ended up being captured and killed. I learned a lot about many foreign countries from her.

I met your dad and your Grandma and Grandpa Ivory at this summer retreat. He came to visit as his mom & dad were there for two weeks. Your dad brought his collie puppy and a friend who owned the ranch where Royal lived. Your dad was planning on buying the ranch of 640 acres near Half Moon Bay. He rented it at this time. He knew that I was a country girl who owned an interest in a ranch so guess that he assumed I'd make him a good wife so he proposed to me in September. I was living in Arcata then as school was in session.

Grandma Ivory had called Royal from camp to come up for a visit as there was someone she wanted him to meet. Me. Your Dad was going through a divorce so she thought I'd make him a good wife and accept the living on the ranch that Royal rented.

When Royal left the camp that summer of 1938, he told me he was going to come up to visit me and do some fishing in the Eel river. He came and I took him fishing for Steel Head at the mouth of the river. I took him to meet my family, Mom, Cele and Cornell and others. By this time I was in my 3rd year of college. I also introduced him to the Brizards. Everyone liked him and I enjoyed doing things with him. I also could bring him to Brizards and to a little house that Lynette and I had Uncle Billy build for us so we had a place to live while going to school. Grandma Paddock came to live there but as I had secured a job with the Brizards, I didn't live in the little house. Uncle Sterl loaned Lynette and me the money to build the house.

I remember a time Royal and I went fishing and I was fishing one hole and he was above me fishing in another hole. I had stopped to change my fly and I heard a cracking sound. I also heard a voice telling me to turn around. I heard the voice twice. I turned around and looked and a tree was falling toward me. I jumped and crouched by a rock that was near me and it missed me but not by very much. The trunk was sort of bare a ways up and when it hit it was rotten inside and it exploded all around me.

Your dad kept coming up to visit me for weekends and courted me with his plans for the future. He invited me to visit his family in San Francisco so I spent a weekend in their apartment there. Royal had invited several young couples to a venison dinner while I was there. After his friends left he proposed to me. He got down on his knees and had a diamond ring that he put on my finger. So I said yes, I would marry him. Royal gave me his fraternity pin to wear so when I went to school, all the kids congratulated me.

We wrote to each other almost every day.

While visiting his family, I met Mary, his sister, and she liked me right away. His mom and dad were all so kind to me.

My art teacher, Stella Little, gave me a shower at her house. She had invited a number of my classmates to the party. It was all so much fun and I enjoyed everything. I almost missed the party that weekend as the invitation had been misplaced by Mrs. Brizard and I didn't get it. I was up on Kneeland with Frances helping her doctor a horse that had cut it's leg on barbed wire. One of the girls at school knew where I had gone so she got a college boy to drive her to Kneeland to find me. They found me and we took off for Arcata to Mrs. Littles home. I was in my old work clothes and smelled like disinfectant but my friends didn't mind. They thought it was just super that I did things like doctoring horses.

I had several engagement parties. One in the little house in Arcata. Mabel Poyfaire was the hostess. Aunt Bertha had a dinner party for me at her home in Eureka. Frances Mullen had a dinner and dance party at Iaqua. She invited half of the people around Kneeland. All the ladies brought food that they served at midnight. She had a money tree instead of gifts. Your dad was there also. He got fed up with the party so we sneaked off without telling anyone but Frances. I always regretted doing this as I felt it wasn't the right thing to do. After this, Royal moved to Reno, Nevada and filed for his divorce. He had already filed for a divorce in California but he wanted to hurry things up so we could get married.

Royal drove all the way from Reno to visit with me for a few days. He wasn't happy that I had so many friends and was involved in many activities where other young men were present. A couple of them were seeing too much of me to suit him. After he put in his 6 weeks in Reno, he asked me to come to Reno and we would get married there. His divorce was final the day we were married. Royal gave me a corsage to wear for our wedding and we had 2 strangers witness our ceremony. I had to buy the wedding ring as Royal was out of funds.

We left Reno right after the service for San Francisco. Our first night was spent at the Ivory's apartment on Knob Hill. Mary wasn't at home so we had her room. We spent a few days there before we headed for Half Moon Bay.

Royal and his first wife lived in the small cabin that he had built on the ranch so that became our first home. A small stream flowed near the cabin so we had plenty of water for a garden and yard. The Steelhead would come up this stream during the spawning season. Everything was green and the flowers were beautiful. I liked this cozy little place. We had a generator for electricity.

Irene Paddock Ivory and Royal A. Ivory

Our many city friends came to visit us. They liked to get the delicious water cress that grew in the little stream there to take home with them. They used it in salads and for sandwiches.

While living in our little house at the end of the canyon I will never forget the afternoon that several sleek black cars came tearing up the road to our house. It was a Saturday so Royal was home. Fred Faustino was there as Royal had invited him to share our dinner that evening. When the cars came to a stop, the men piled out. Some had uniform type of clothing and some were dressed in black. Your dad said "It's some federal men. They must be lost".

I had a flash of concern come to my mind. Sterl had sent us a package of venison jerky which was against the law to have at that time of year. Sterl had written on the return address of the package, "From your Uncle Dudley". Maybe they thought we had received a shipment of drugs and the Post Office had informed them of this queer return address.

I grabbed the package papers and jerky and put it in my washing machine with clothes piled on top.

It turned out that they were looking for drugs and had papers saying that we were being charged with the growing of drugs and they had a search warrant. Search they did, but all they got from their efforts was nettle stings.

The Wurlitzers, the piano Wurlitzers, came often to visit us as Mrs. Wurlitzer liked water cress to serve her city friends. They enjoyed bringing picnic food to share with us and their children loved the outdoor freedom at our place. Everyone enjoyed this quiet, peaceful setting as the cabin was snuggled at the foot of the mountains. Huge eucalyptus trees grew along the mile long road that led to our retreat.

First home of Royal and Irene Ivory at Half Moon Bay

The only other human, besides us, lived about a half mile down the canyon from us. It was Fred Faustino, a Portugese immigrant, whom Royal was negotiating to buy the ranch from. He was an old bachelor so we took pity on him and had him share many a meal with us. We also took him on several fishing trips.

After 3 years, I became pregnant with Gayle so we didn't include Fred in our activities so much. Gayle was born while we lived in the little house. When I was about 5 months pregnant with Gayle, one time I had to lug water up the mountain to a cow that had given birth and was sick. The cow was a young animal and it was her first calf. Fred had pulled the calf and thus she was injured. We had a veterinarian come but he couldn't help the cow, so she died. I really had a struggle carrying the heavy bucket of water and I felt sad because that beautiful, young, white faced mother had died.

We decided we needed more room as our family grew. We built a larger house that was near the highway. This was in 1942 and when the war broke out Royal didn't want to join the Army so he convinced Fred to let us sell the ranch so Royal could take a job with the Pitt River Power Company near Mt. Shasta.

We left Fred Faustino to look after the place while we went to Mr. Shasta where Royal got his job interview and he was hired at $140 a month with a home to live in as part of the job.

We had about 40 head of Hereford Cattle that we put up for sale. We had bought a bull from Mr. Keystone, a luggage tycoon, that had a ranch not far from our place. He bought all our cattle. The Keystones were very friendly people who had us for many a dinner when they were down from the city to see about their ranch. They also had us for several dinners at their San Francisco home. I think that having Grandpa Harry Ivory as part of our family gave us a little prestige with some of these wealthy families as he was the Personnel Manager for the Standard Oil Company and had charge of 7 western states.

Royal H. Ivory, Irene Paddock Ivory, Adeline Flint Ivory and Royal A. Ivory

During our stay in Half Moon Bay, I sold my share of our Kneeland Ranch to Sterling for $2000 and sold my share in the little house in Arcata to Lynette for $500. We used the money to buy our cattle. Mr. Keystone paid us $4000 for our herd of white faces.

Fred let us sell the ranch, all 640 acres, except for a few acres around his cabin as he didn't want to move. Royal and I took off for Shasta to look at some land that was for sale. We left our Collie dog, Foxy, with Fred to take care of while we were gone. We also left a baby calf in his care. After being gone for 3 days, we arrived home at sundown. To our horror we found a starved calf and dog that welcomed us with much barking and bawling. We knew something was wrong and our first thought was that Fred had been injured, so Royal took off up the canyon to check on Fred at his cabin. In the meantime I fed the dog and calf. Royal came down the road to our house driving very fast. He jumped out of the car and said, "My God, Irene , Fred is dead. There is blood everywhere." We both agreed that the Sheriff should be contacted so Royal drove to the town of Half Moon Bay and the authorities followed him back to Fred's cabin. They found Fred sitting in a chair with his shotgun strapped to his arm. He had shot himself in his head. Parts of his head were blown all around the room. A scene of horror for Royal.

We contacted Fred's 2 nieces of this tragedy. They lived in a town further south so didn't arrive until the next day. They took over his funeral arrangements. We had a contract with Fred to buy his ranch for $10,000. This we paid to his nieces and proceeded to finalize our sale of the ranch to the buyer who had put some earnest money on the deal. We did this sale in preparation for moving to Mt. Shasta. I was pregnant with Garf so moved to Grandma Ivory's home in San Francisco. Grandpa Ivory had passed away shortly before Garf was born so she welcomed having me and Gayle there as Royal had moved to Mr. Shasta to begin his new job at the power plant. Garf was born in San Mateo, California. Garf was 12 days old when we moved to the Pitt River Power House. This is where your dad learned how to operate a power plant.

We were given a very nice house to live in while we were there. A very nice lawn surrounded the house and there were some flowers and shrubs. Many other families also lived in this small community. They all worked for the power company.

One evening after Royal came home from work he decided to check out the 410 shotgun as some of the men were going bird hunting and asked him to go along. Royal was loading the gun and it accidently went off with a loud blast. Many of our neighbors came running over to see if anyone was hurt. They thought Royal had shot me. Garf was in his crib but Gayle and I were near. The lead went through the wall above the front door so no one was injured. The other men went hunting without Royal. One young man offered to teach your dad how to load and unload a gun. Your dad was a fisherman, fly fishing to be exact, and he had no desire to go deer hunting.

The deer population was extensive. Several Mule Tail Deer got into the over flow of water above the power plant and slid down the spill-way which resulted in their deaths.

Our neighbors always shared some of their venison with us. It was always a treat for us and sure helped our food budget.

We stayed about a year at Pitt #1 power house and then Royal was transferred to another power house several miles down the Pitt River. There were only about 7 families living there. the company moved us into a larger and much nicer home when we had been there for a year.

While living in this house, the company re-roofed the house. Garf loved to pick up the fallen shingles after the workers left for the day. All of a sudden I heard Garf coughing and choking so I ran into the living room area and saw Garf standing there looking so startled like something had happened. He couldn't tell me what was wrong. When I saw he had several shingle nails in his hands I assumed he had swallowed one. So I immediately took him into the kitchen and filled him up on bread, especially the crusts. The next morning we took him into town and had him x-rayed and sure enough he had 2 shingle nails going point down inside his bowels. The doctor could be called an old country doctor today. He told me to keep feeding him dry foods like bread and potatoes and bring him in again the next day. We took Garf in early the next morning and found from the x-ray that the nails had moved through much of the bowels with no problem. It was necessary for me to keep Garf quiet and watch for the nails in his stool. It worked. The next morning they were eliminated in his stool. I was so relieved. It wasn't easy for the roofers to work when a family was living there, especially with an open ceiling to contend with. They had torn out the water stained plaster board ceiling so it made quite a mess and they weren't too careful in cleaning up before leaving for the night.

There were lots of small animals living in and around this small group of homes. At night the porcupines would come out to eat grass on our lawn. You could hear them chomping and chewing away. If they disturbed my sleep I would get out of bed and go to the open window and listen to them as they filled their bellies. In the morning they were all gone. A few fruit trees grew around each house so the ring-tailed cats or opossum came to eat apples as the raccoons did. Occasionally a few deer would wander through our camp and enjoy eating the apples. There were lots of chipmunks and gray squirrels. Gayle and Garf always enjoyed watching them scamper up and down the trees.

FALL RIVER MILLS

We moved to Fall River Mills from Half Moon Bay.

One of the hardest chores there that I had to do was washing clothes by hand as we didn't have a washing machine. In the laundry area there was a double sink with hot and cold running water. I would put the clothes in one side to soak in hot water and soap. Then I used a scrubbing board to wash them. I rinsed them several times to get the dirt and soap out. Then I hung them outside on a long clothes line. It would take me all day to get the washing done. The next day I pressed and ironed all the clothes. Garf was still a baby so I had his diapers and clothes to wash separately. It seemed like I did nothing but wash clothes. The bedding was the most difficult to keep clean. I had no one to help me.

Aunt Ida, Uncle Gil and Mary came to visit when we lived there so I spent a lot of time before they came just washing, ironing and cleaning everything. It was so nice to have company and I enjoyed them so much. It was November and Gayle had her third birthday while they were there. I made a dinner for her with an angel food cake for dessert. Aunt Ida gave Gayle a xylophone for a present so we had music much of the time. Aunt Ida spent some time teaching Gayle how to play the xylophone. She loved this toy.

I had ordered Gayle a papoose for her birthday from an old Indian lady and it would have an Indian doll inside it. It was the kind of basket that the babies were in as the Indian women carried them on their backs. Gayle never got her Indian basket because Royal sent the old Indian lady away when she came to deliver it to me. I never paid her for it and she never came to visit me again.

Gayle's third birthday with her plaid skirt and xylophone

While living in the Pitt River Camp, we had a milk cow so I did the milking. The cream came in handy for making butter and other goodies like whip cream for cakes. I also fed, watered, and staked the cow out where she could get fresh grass. It added a lot of extra work for myself, but I rather enjoyed it as Gayle and Garf liked to go with me. They enjoyed the cow also.

When Garf was 3 weeks old we went camping with another family that worked with Royal at the plant. The place we set up camp was a miserable location. Gayle fell off the plank bridge which spanned a small stream. I was worried so much that she had sucked some of the mud in her mouth and nose as she fell flat on her face. It was a real chore getting her clean and also taking care of a hungry baby. Royal helped get Gayle up on the bank and that is where his help had ended. The men were busy getting their fishing gear ready so they could go and try their luck the next morning.

We slept in the station wagon for 3 nights. I had to hold Garf up close to me to keep him warm as it had rained and the swampy location of our camp wasn't pleasant.

The family that we were camping with had a little girl about Gayle's age so they enjoyed each others companionship. I was thankful for that. Garf was a good baby and didn't cry or fuss very much. To get his milk warm was very difficult especially in the middle of the night. My banging with a camp stove was noisy so it did disturb the other family. Since I didn't nurse Garf, I had this problem as you can't feed a tiny little boy cold milk.

The men didn't get enough fish to feed all of us. I cooked bacon and made hash brown potatoes out of the boiled potatoes that I took. We ate a lot of snack food on that trip.

On one of our fishing trips, I almost had an encounter with a bear who was also fishing the stream we were on. It was called Bear Creek. I heard a lot of noises in the bushes and something like slapping in the water. Then I knew there was a bear so I sneaked away and informed Royal. We decided to leave Bear Creek to the bears. This had been the 4th camping trip that bears were around the area that we were.

We had a bear problem when we took Grandpa Harry with us for a week of camping and fishing before we moved from Half Moon Bay. At night they came into our camp and Grandpa Ivory was sleeping in the tent. Royal and I slept in the station wagon. The next morning we saw their paw marks in the dirt around the tent and station wagon. We didn't have the children at that time. I don't think Grandpa enjoyed the trip.

GRANTS PASS, OREGON

We sold our herd of white face cattle when we moved to Fall River Mills so had a little nest egg of about $6,000. This was good as we moved to Grants Pass, Oregon. We bought a ten acre place with an old log house on the upper part of the land just above the main highway. The lower part of the land boarded on the Rogue River where Royal sometimes fished. He wasn't too successful in catching any fish there. Clark Gable had a place just up the road from our home. We would wave at him when we'd walk by and he was friendly and would wave back.

The old man that we bought the place from let his milk goats live in the house with him so consequently we had quite a lot of work to do to repair the plaster walls that the goats had damaged with their horns. The floors in some rooms were covered with goat dung. I had quite a job cleaning it out. I used a wash of Lysol soap and water which sterilized it.

While we were cleaning all this we lived at a local motel. Eddie Nunn was the owner of the motel and he let us keep our cat. I had a box of dirt for the cat and put newspapers under it. The owners were very good to us and became our friends. Later on when the Eddie's wife got very sick, they asked me to run the motel for them while he took her to some doctors who were specialists in the San Francisco area. They paid me a good salary so we had money for food and also a room for our use. Gayle and Garf were so good. They had a small park area so played there while I worked.

Royal's sister Mary came to visit us and rode the train to get to what we called our goat house and stayed a couple weeks. I remember washing Gayle and Garf in the laundry tubs when she was there. Mary washed her hair in the tubs too and she used vinegar water to make her hair shine. It was so pretty. We invited Frank and Ruth Sullivan to ham dinner while Mary was with us.

Frank and Ruth were our good friends for a long time. One day Garf was sitting on the sofa next to Frank. Garf was about 2 years old then. Garf sure liked Frank and would put his little hand on Frank's leg. One day he pinched Frank's leg and Frank said "By God, what do you teach this boy Irene?". Then he told me it wasn't the first time Garf had pinched him. They didn't have any children and were always good to us. Ruth gave Gayle a beautiful Scotch plaid outfit that had straps that went over her shoulder for her birthday.

Royal and I took a couple of days away from family cares. We left Gayle and Garf with Mary. She took them out to a small stream for some fun. They had water fights and splashed and played in the water and then had a picnic lunch. Garf drank some of the stream water and got very sick with a high fever of 105 degrees. When we got home, Mary was beside herself. She didn't know what to do. We took Garf to the doctor and I never did know what he had contacted but with some medicine and lots of care, he soon was back to being himself. I did enjoy having Mary visit us.

Royal was working for a real estate company. They trained him and gave him materials to study so he could take the realtor test. He passed the test so the company kept him on the payroll but he wasn't too successful and became discouraged and quit. He went to work for a landscape nursery.

While working at the nursery, Royal met a man who was selling prefabricated homes. Royal worked out a deal with him to build a house at a reduced price which could be used as a display home. It became our "Home Ola" which was what these houses were called. Royal became a salesman for the company and he had 15 families who wanted to buy these houses. The city of Grants Pass determined that they wouldn't give permits to build this type of house. They claimed that the houses wouldn't pass inspection so that was the end of that adventure.

Eileen was born when we lived in the Home Ola. Mary came to stay with us so Gayle and Garf would have someone they knew to take care of them.

Mary had been an ambulance driver for the 2nd World War. She had picked up injured men from the ships that docked in San Francisco. The war ended and so did Mary's job. We sure welcomed her with open arms as it really help us a lot.

The Home Ola was small so not convenient when we had extra family with us. It was hard for Mary. She had a sofa bed to sleep on and it wasn't anything that I was proud to own.

Mary was with us for about 2 weeks and her cousin, Uncle Gil's son, came to visit her then. He had a crush on Mary. To our complete surprise she let him convince her to go back to San Francisco. That of course was the end to her helping us out.

When Royal came home he was very mad at Mary as we were expecting our baby any day. Royal packed a few clothes and headed for Eureka, California to get my mother to come and help us out. He drove all night and when he got to Eureka he slept for a couple of hours while Mom packed some clothes for a stay at our place. I was so happy to see her as I knew the baby would soon be here. I went to the hospital that night and was very thankful for Mom's help.

Eileen was born in the late hours of the night. Since this was just after the war, the hospital was very short on help. There were no registered nurses. The practical nurses that were there told me to hold the baby back as the doctor was exhausted and had to have a couple hours of sleep. They gave me a shot of some drug that just put me out cold. Before the nurse gave me the shot, I told her the baby was going to come and begged her to get the doctor. No dice. I told Royal to get the doctor but he wouldn't do it. I was completely out of this world when Eileen was born. After the doctor came they tried to wake me out of the drugged condition but I couldn't respond. They slapped my face and put cold water on my face and none of it helped. I know they used forceps and had a very difficult time helping Eileen get born.

When 10 days passed and I could go home, the nurse brought Eileen in to see me. I asked to see the doctor before I left the hospital. I told him that there was something wrong with my baby and I wanted him to check her over. It just felt like something wasn't right with Eileen. The first time he checked her he didn't find anything wrong. Then when I was all ready to go home, the nurse brought Eileen in dressed in her cute little white dress. While I was sitting there waiting for Royal to come, I noticed something different about her. I refused to leave until the doctor did a thorough examination. He did. This time he picked up on the heart beat. The doctor put her in an oxygen covered crib and she was there for a month. We found out that she had a defective heart and I was told that I might find her dead in her crib sometime. I would check her every night many times and I never knew what to expect. My Mom was a big help at this time and her 3 weeks spent with us was a blessing.

I didn't have a crib for Eileen so I put her in a cedar chest that my Uncle Billy had made for me. She had to stay there until we could afford a bed for Garf and give her his crib. Royal was in and out of work and we were very poor. Eileen was about 8 months old when we managed a second hand bed for Garf.

One day while we lived in the Home Ola Garf was riding his hobby horse and it would bounce backwards. He was overly strong and with one quick rock he hit the side of the kitchen stove and cut his tongue all the way thru in half with his teeth. It was about 9 o'clock at night and Royal stayed with Gayle and Eileen while I took Garf to the hospital. There was one nurse and one doctor on duty. Because of the shortage of medical personnel, the doctor asked me to help him sew Garf's tongue. I held the clamps on his tongue while the nurse gave him an anesthetic. It didn't take too long to repair the damage. Garf was so good thru all of this and I did have some pain medicine that helped. His tongue healed in a few days and he never sucked his thumb again.

We sold the Home Ola and bought 10 acres on the outskirts of Grants Pass where we built a house that we lived in until we moved from there to Othello in 1952. We rented a home while we were building the new house. Mom and Bertram Betterley were married in our rented house there in Grants Pass.

While we were living in the rented home waiting for our new home to be completed, Gayle and Royal had the red measles. Royal ended up in the hospital for a few days. Gayle had a very high fever of 106 degrees and there were 2 doctors that would drop in and see her every day until her fever went down. We had to keep the curtains closed all day to keep the light out while she was sick.

Royal and I were building our home on the 10 acre section of land. It was quite close to the city and a school for the 3 children.

We built a very nice home with hard wood floors. The birds eye maple floors in our new home were purchased from the extra wood that had been purchased for the school gym floor. They had ordered too much for the gym floor so we purchased the excess and used it for our flooring. I had given it 2 coats of finishing and it was a beautiful floor. We didn't have money for carpets or new furniture. We had no drapes or curtains.

We leased the lower field across the ditch and in front of the new house to gladiola flower growers. When they bloomed it was like a sea of beautiful color.

Gayle and Garf with baby goats

Grandpa Betterly water witched for the location of our well. It did produce water but not too much so we had to be careful how we used it.

Royal was the principal at the Merlin School. Gayle rode to Merlin school each day with her dad. Gayle was in the 1st and 2nd and part of 3rd grade there and Miss Grisswold was her teacher.

While living at the 10 acre ranch, we raised calves, goats, ducks and I kept a neighbors pet rabbits for awhile. There were also some chickens that I raised there. I milked the goats and we used the milk for drinking. I wasn't keen on it nor were Gayle and Garf. Chocolate syrup helped to change the taste so they would drink it. We had to borrow a billy goat for breeding our nannies and he sure smelled bad. It was quite a chore having him at the ranch for the couple of weeks it took for breeding. The baby goats that were born were so cute and playful. Gayle, Garf and Eileen loved to play with the little goats and named them. One white one was called Snow White.

Gayle had entered a local contest and won a registered Collie Dog that was related to the dog that was Lassie in the movies. She named it Gayle's Cuff and one day Cuff got killed while chasing a flock of quail across the country road by our house. A taxi driver hit her as she was crossing the road. He came to the house to tell me and helped carry her to where I buried her. He said he was sorry but admitted he was speeding and couldn't stop in time. I wrapped Cuff in a blanket and got the shovel and took Eileen with me to dig the hole to bury her. I cried most of the time while I was digging that grave and Eileen was only about 2 years old and really didn't quite know why I cried. As she watched me she petted Cuff's head and said poor doggie is sleeping. I wanted to get her buried before Gayle and Garf came home from school. I showed them her grave but it was hard for them to understand why. They put flowers on the grave every day for a long while.

I trained hops for a season in Grants Pass. It was a very hard job as I had Eileen to care for. That was when George and May Loghry came into our lives. George and May lived down the road from our new home and their daughter took care of Eileen while I had this job. Gayle and Garf were in school.

Fruitdale School was down the road. Gayle started there during her 3rd grade year and Garf went there for the second half of his 1st grade. His first part of the year was at Merlin with Mr. Mahoney as his teacher.

I also picked raspberries for a neighbor. I could take Eileen with me since the owner had a little girl that Eileen could play with. We only picked in the early hours of the morning.

One of Royal's students, Clara Nell, baby sat for us and lived with us when we were thinning Red Delicious apples in the Dalles, Oregon area. Royal also worked for the orchardists. They had 1 room cottages for the workers with running water outside and a stove and sink inside. Toilets were outside. It was very primitive and not a happy situation for a teenage girl. She was always good help to me and very cheerful. Royal spent every afternoon and evening fishing in streams around the area. The owners of the orchard were friendly to us and my first rides in an Army Jeep were there with this family. The man drove us all around his orchard and took us to town once. I enjoyed the jeep rides.

When the apples were all thinned and that job done, we stayed for awhile and weeded the owners vegetable garden for them. While I was doing the weeding, the children washed their clothes in the sink and Clara Nell helped them do that job. They took showers in the shower stall that was outside by the bathrooms. I know that Gayle, Garf, Eileen, and I were very thankful to be back in our new home.

Garf, Eileen, and Gayle on Eileen's 3rd birthday at the new home in Grant's Pass, Oregon

One afternoon I was looking out our kitchen window and I saw a pack of about 7 dogs chasing a deer down the slope on the hill behind us. They had taken chunks of her hind legs out as they jumped and grabbed her with their teeth. I opened the door and yelled at them but that didn't stop their mad attack. We had been told by our neighbors to be very careful if we ever went up in the hills as the dogs might attack us and they were obviously very vicious.

We didn't have the luxury of a phone. There was a grocery store near us and the owner let me charge food if I didn't have enough money to pay for it. At the end of the month, I usually didn't have any money so I really appreciated the store owner trusting me.

Royal and I sold Miracle Maid Cookware for awhile. Royal thought it would help us to get rich and fell for the project. I bought food and prepared it all for cooking at the hosts home. We had ham, sweet potatoes, and a vegetable and I also made pancakes which I served with butter and syrup. I also demonstrated how to make an upside down pineapple cake in a fry pan. I always served coffee from the Miracle Maid coffeepot. When we traveled to Eureka to visit my mother and sister Lucille, I would take Eileen and go out canvassing for business. I still have some of the cookware and use it but the aluminum scare came along then and people were afraid to buy it. It was a lot of hard work. Gayle was eleven years old and old enough to take care of Garf and Eileen when we went out in the evening to do our demonstrations. I cooked while Royal gave a talk explaining how wonderful this method of cooking was. We usually sold enough to pay for the food and got to purchase our cookware at a reduced price.

Grandma Ivory visited us once when we lived in the new house. She criticized my lack of furnishing the house. She said she would do certain things to improve the looks of our home. She just couldn't seem to understand that her dear son didn't earn much money. There were many times that I had to charge groceries or we wouldn't have had anything to eat. It made me feel bad especially when she told me I should learn how to spend the money. Royal tried many things but he never was a good provider. I didn't purchase cosmetics or many clothes and I never had hand cream to use for myself or lotion for the children. We were always poor. I never accused Royal about not earning enough money and I think he just didn't know what to do. He always wanted me to decide what to do. When he was teaching we managed much better and so when we lived in Grants Pass, he went to Southern Oregon State College in Ashland to get his teaching degree. Royal graduated from Southern Oregon College and secured a job as principal for the Merlin School.

Royal met a woman at college named Mary Jane Blood that had an operation on her colon and he felt sorry for her. He invited her to dinner and to spend a weekend with us. She could eat only certain foods and I didn't know what to cook. I had a roasted ham and served corn which didn't work well for her because of her colostomy.

I was required by Royal to serve quite a few dinners for him and his guests. They always turned out okay but it always ruined the food budget. There were never many treats for the children. I did make cakes and pies etc. but the usual treats were never in the budget. Sometimes I would splurge and buy ice cream. I made root beer floats in the summer and Gayle, Garf, and Eileen really liked that. They never begged for anything and I was thankful for that.

I remember that Garf used to ask me to make rash (hash). He would ask "When are you going to make rash again, Mom?". I just thought this was so nice. None of them ever complained and they just accepted what I could do.

When Dewey was running for President of the United States, he stopped in Grants Pass so Royal and I went to see him and listen to his speech. We shook his hand after introducing ourselves. That was the only time I was ever close to a famous political person.

I took some classes at Southern Oregon in Ashland also. Each day I would take my children, Gayle, Garf, and Eileen, with me to school. The college had classes that the children could attend. At lunch time we would all go to the park and eat our lunch and look at the park animals. They enjoyed the monkeys the most. I don't know what kept Royal busy while the family was gone. I hated the drive home each evening because the sun was always in my eyes.

Mr. Larson, the old man who lived in a little house above ours, was always bringing us a bottle of his home made wine. His wife never came with him. One day he told us that his stomach hurt him all the time and the wine seemed to help him. On a visit another day after that he told us that the wine didn't help him anymore so we suggested that he see a doctor. He wanted Eileen's hospital so we gave his daughter the address of the Stanford Lane Hospital and she got an appointment with a specialist there. The doctors did an exploratory operation and found he had cancer all through his body. He came home to die. I would visit him almost every day as he was bed ridden. His wife begged me to come and see him and I felt so sorry for him. All I could do was try to encourage him and give him some cheer.

OTHELLO, WASHINGTON

Royal was fired from his job at Merlin. We had to do something. I didn't earn enough and couldn't find a steady job. I tried but when prospective employers saw that I had a little child they declined to offer me a job. Royal tried to get me a job. I was interviewed for a teaching job and rejected and told to stay home and take care of my children.

Royal heard about the irrigation going in all around the Columbia Basin area. We sold our home and moved to Othello Washington. He had heard such fantastic things about getting rich raising onions etc. The only reason we got a farm unit was because Aunt Cele and Uncle Bill sold us a strip of land just above the unit we got. We paid the $400.00 for it. That gave us the power to buy our unit. All had to be approved by the Farmers Home Association.

Earl Taylor loaned us a trailer to live in as we had no place to stay. Rental housing didn't exist in Othello. We stayed in the trailer for awhile until a small apartment became available. For a few nights we stayed at Aunt Cele's cabin and then pitched a tent for a few nights as well just before we were able to move into the apartment. The apartment had 1 bedroom for all 5 of us.

Garf was in the 3rd grade and Gayle in the 5th grade when they started school at Othello that year. The old brick building that was once the school has now been demolished and the football field now takes its place.

Mary and Wilbur Phelps came to visit us from Half Moon Bay. They weren't too impressed with the country around. Mary helped me fix food for all of us. Mary and Wilbur weren't getting along too well and after they got back home they filed for divorce. Wilbur didn't want any children and Mary did. Her time clock was ticking away and I never heard from Mary again. Wilbur wrote to me a couple times after Royal and I separated. He married again to a woman who had 3 grown sons. I liked Mary so I felt sad that she didn't write to me after her divorce.

The couple and their children whose rabbits we took care of in Grants Pass came to Othello to visit us. The little girl liked Gayle a lot and I cannot remember their names. We didn't have accommodations for visitors so they didn't stay long.

Mary and George Loghry were the only old friends who moved to Othello and stayed there.

I got a job working for the Superintendent of Schools just a couple weeks after we arrived in Othello.

We bought our farm unit and obtained our FHA loan to build a house on the land. First we built a shed that we moved into while doing the building of our house. We had no running water so we hauled water from Mom and Bert's place. I took our laundry up there as well and sometimes went to a Laundromat in town. It was such a chore to just keep us all clean. The shed was cold in the winter time and wasn't pleasant. We did have electricity so used a couple of space heaters. I put bricks in the oven to heat them up and then wrapped them in towels to put in the beds so the children could have warm feet. The toilet was outside and the children hated to go down there when it was so cold.

Garf started his farming career at the age of eight. He and Gayle learned how to drive the tractor, start irrigation tubes, and take care of the farm animals.

We had our land leveled and irrigation water started to wet the soil before planting. The soil was very dry and the ditches would break out and we had problems patching them. Once I was up to my waist in the ditch trying to patch a hole that the ground squirrels had dug. It was 2 o'clock in the morning. At first we had to keep a close check on the water. I was so tired I felt like a zombie walking around and I would almost fall asleep at my desk at the school building. I earned $150 a month which fed us and paid the bills. Royal was busy developing the farm. This was about 1953.

While living there we raised a vegetable garden, chickens, pigs and cattle and the crops on the land. We also had a franchise with Western Farmers to sell farm products to the local farmers. I kept the books for this business. When we sold over a hundred thousand dollars of their products they decided it was too big for us to handle so we lost the dealership.

When it came time to kill the animals for our winter food, I had to do the killing. Since I had been raised on a farm I could do it. I hated the job of killing the chickens and I was told to kill the turkeys too, so I tried. They were big and hard to handle. I tied their 2 feet together and strung them up on a rope but when it came to killing them I just quit. I just couldn't do that. Well I put an add in the paper to sell all the turkeys we had and I bought a turkey from the store for Thanksgiving. We had invited May and George Loghry to share our dinner that Thanksgiving and we had a very pleasant time and my mind was thankful.

One of our Herford yearlings dropped over dead from bloat so we got Uncle Bill to come down and skin it out so the meat was okay. He bled it first which is necessary and he knew how to do it since he had worked at a butcher shop for years in California. With the pigs we hired a local man to do the butchering for us.

I missed the turkey eggs after the turkeys were gone. They are just as good as hens eggs for cooking. We had a few Bante chickens running around our farm to keep the bugs out of the garden. Eileen enjoyed these little chickens a lot. I refused to kill and eat them or would never serve them to the children.

I milked Ginger, our cow, morning and night and made butter from the cream. Gayle and Garf help me do the churning. After Royal left I sold the milk to a couple of teachers who were happy to get it and mostly because it was rich in cream. I finally sold Ginger and was thankful that I didn't have to do any more milking. It was a hard chore in the morning when I had to get ready to go to work and rush, rush to do it all.

The children and I kept the garden weeded and watered. Royal used the tractor to disc up the land for planting.

If the cattle broke out of the electric fence, Royal would use the car to chase them back. He could drive the car almost anywhere over the farm as it wasn't too rugged or steep.

When Gayle was 11 years old, Royal made her drive the car to town. I knew she was frightened but she did as she was told. She had learned how to drive when she herded the cattle with the car. She made it in and back safely. It was only about 5 miles to town and 5 miles back.

Just before we got the doors on the house, I came home from my job one day to find a large gray snake in the living room. I used my kitchen broom to scoot him out and then I asked Garf if he had put the snake in the house. He said no but for a long time I thought that is how the snake got into the house. Years later I asked Garf about it again and he said the he didn't do it. I felt bad about accusing him. I was just thankful that it wasn't a rattle snake.

We had lots of scorpions, small ones, and that worried me a lot. We found black widow spiders around too. Rabbits were quite thick on the farm.

Royal caught a baby rabbit and brought it home for the children to raise. Well guess what—it got out of its box and hid under the hot water heater. We had quite the time trying to get it out. We didn't succeed but it did come out the next day so I was able to catch it. It just didn't live long as it was a wild rabbit and probably scared to death and missed its mother. We really didn't know how to take care of it.

Ben Caylor flew Royal and me to Lake Chelan for a vacation trip so Royal could do some fishing. I enjoyed this trip. Ben picked us up when the time came for us to head for home. Grandma Ivory was with us when we took these few days off. She took care of the kids. They sure enjoyed her bread pudding. I really didn't want to go and leave Grandma Ivory alone with the kids but Royal insisted. She was stuck out there on the farm

Gayle, Eileen, and Garf at Grand Coulee Dam in 1953

with no car to drive as it was parked at Caylor's place. There wasn't much in the line of food for her to cook either. I really felt bad about leaving her there. Ben flew her down to Portland as part of her trip home to San Francisco. It was evidently a rugged flight as the winds were strong. Grandmother Ivory always managed to get to see us no matter where we lived.

Ben only made a few trips with his little plane after this as he put his little plane to rest. The last trip he made he was unable to land the plane because of strong winds. He flew around Othello for quite awhile and decided to try and land and flew into some building and did a lot of damage to his plane. Ben had been an Air Force pilot in World War 1.

When we got our home finished, life was more pleasant. Now we had a bathroom, laundry room and 3 bedrooms. Garf and Gayle helped to put the roof on and Garf did many other farm chores while we were building.

Royal wasn't happy so we went to Spokane for some counseling. First it was family counseling. The counselors told me that they couldn't handle Royal and recommended a specialist. They told me he was too hot to handle. I attended 1 session with him but Royal went to several. When this was all over he took a trip to Banff, Canada, alone. He also took some dancing lessons in Spokane at the Arthur Murray Dance Studio there. I was unaware of these things he was planning until I received the bill from the dance studio for $300. I confronted Royal about it and I suggested that I would like to join him and take some dancing lessons too. This didn't take.

His trip to Banff, Canada was a surprise to me too and when I knew what he had planned I suggested that we take the whole family for a vacation. He went alone and when he got home he bragged about meeting a lady that could really dance.

Well, somehow we kept the home fires burning and took care of the farm and irrigation. Gayle and Garf had helped me with everything. They deserved some kind words for what they had done.

Royals school friend Lorene and her husband Phil came to visit us in Othello. Their two girls were also with them. While they were here, Royal drove them all around and took them to see Grand Coulee Dam. That was when he decided he wanted Lorene to leave her husband and be his love. He had dated

Lorene when they were in high school. When they went home she send a large box of clothes to Gayle. Things that her daughters had outgrown.

Royal was really sneaky with his correspondence to Lorene but I discovered where he hid her letters and the ones he was writing to her. He put them in the book that was large and one that contained family history. It was a book that the family didn't look through very often.

Royal's next trip took him to California to see Lorene. That is when I interfered with a letter to her friend asking her to talk with Lorene. She did so and Lorene cut off her letters to Royal and she apologized to me. That didn't work out like Royal wanted.

The children had a lot of chores to do as we developed the farm. Gayle and Garf learned how to drive the tractor and use the irrigation tubes. Gayle helped me in the house a lot and ironed some of our clothes. Garf irrigated the crops.

I will never forget the day that a farmer brought us several little pigs that we had purchased from him. The pen that Royal built wasn't very strong so the next day those little rascals got out and we had a merry chase trying to catch them. We chased them and chased them and laughed and laughed. We were exhausted by the time they were safe in their pen again.

We had left Grants Pass in 1952 to move to Othello and Royal left us in 1956 for Portland Oregon. At first he told me that he would come back for us as soon as he got established.

Royal had received $14,000.00 from Aunt Florence McMurtries' estate. That sparked things up for them. Aunt Florence had left me $500 which certainly helped me at the time.

I only met Aunt Florence and Uncle Terry McMurtrie two times. They came to San Francisco to see us and then to Grants Pass, Oregon. I always felt sad to think that we never would get to Pittsburgh, Pennsylvania to visit with them. Royal did take Harriet back to see Aunt Florence after he and Harriet were married.

Royal never did come back for us so things were left in my hands. I had the job at school which made the interest payment to the FHA and the rest went for food and gas. Royal took our new station wagon and left us with an ancient worn out Pontiac (a 1948) that kept breaking down. Since we lived 5 miles out of town it was necessary to have a car that ran. Garf built a ramp with planks so I could back the car up the planks. That way I could get enough momentum in the morning to get the car started. There was a side window missing so when the cold weather started it was so cold to ride in it.

I complained via the phone to Royal about the car so he brought us a slightly newer used Plymouth (a 1953) which kept us from being recluses on the farm.

Garf built a spot next to the shed for the car. He used straw bales which helped to keep the car from freezing. One day that car just gave out as it was a tired old car. I called an auto shop in Ellensburg and asked them to bring me a car that would run and would last for awhile. We had done business with the owner of the shop so knew him. He brought us a much better car to use and the payments weren't too much. It lasted for awhile until Garf ran over a rock on the road that broke something underneath the car. We sure had a lot of old cars and a lot of trouble with them.

I started teaching and I was able to buy a new car which was such a blessing. Royal was supposed to send me $50 a month for each child for support which he very seldom did. It was very tough making the payments on the farm and car and sometimes we were lucky to have enough money at the end of the month to buy a loaf of bread.

Eric had loaned me his car to drive to Ritzville to finalize my divorce from Royal. Royal had found a new woman in Portland.

He had met Lee and lived with her. She was a nice lady and concerned about us. Lee was at the Childrens hospital in Seattle with Royal when Eileen had her 2nd open heart operation. She ate lunch with me one day and asked me a lot of questions about Royal. She especially wanted to know about his temper. This didn't work out with Lee. Then he met Harriet where he taught school.

Harriet wasn't in a happy marriage so Royal convinced her to leave her husband and when she became divorced and free, she married him.

As Garf grew he became an expert mechanic by repairing farm equipment and building drag racing cars. He started this about age 14. He already knew how to mow, rake and bale hay and assumed most of the responsibilities on our 90 acre farm.

We were $26,000.00 in debt to the FHA and farm bills when Royal left us. He sold our insurance policy for $4 to $5 thousand dollars and sent me

$1 thousand as our share. It helped pay our bills and I sold the few head of cattle we had along with our milk cow which brought in $1 thousand dollars to pay the FHA and other farm bills.

My Uncle Billy fell off a roof he was repairing and it killed him. I inherited $1 thousand dollars from his estate. These were God sent dollars which helped me a lot. I used some of the money for college as I had to get a degree in order to keep teaching. Sterling, my brother, also loaned me $3500 to pay FHA and farm bills. I rented the farm land to the Carlson brothers for one year which helped us.

Garf worked some for Marvin Carlson so he had money for his needs. None of us had much to spend on clothes or much of anything else.

George Loghry was a big help to me. He helped Garf farm by cutting the hay as I didn't have any equipment. When Garf was 16 I did buy a new Allis Chalmer tractor and some hay equipment for Garf to use. Garf did custom baling for our neighbors with the new tractor.

One night Garf was moving the tractor and equipment and a pick-up full of kids ran into him. They were teenage boys that had all been up at the base where they could get beer to drink. They were all crowded into the pick up so it was hard driving. The parents sued us so Garf and I had to go to court in Ritzville. We proved that we weren't to blame so it didn't cost us anything. Garf had installed lights on the tractor so it could be seen much better before the accident which helped. The impact with the pickup and tractor threw Garf off and he avoided getting run over by the tractor by rolling himself down the road away from the wreckage.

Eric Strom had seen Gayle walking in Othello one day and he told his Air Force buddies that she was the girl he was going to marry. Eric was in the Air Force and stationed at the 637th Radar Base. Eric wasn't any better off than we were. He had an old car too. He kept it running by fixing it a lot.

Gayle graduated from Othello High School with honors and planned to go to college at Washington State College. She started that fall. Eric and Gayle wrote to each other and she was still dating Jay Steensma at that time. When she was sent home because of her back problem, she was put in traction in the Othello Hospital. Eric brought some roses and visited her there. He was a persistent wooer.

One day he invited Gayle to go to Wenatchee to meet his Mom. They got married in East Wenatchee with the help of Eric's mother Margie. I didn't know what was going on until they came home and said they were married. Eric was scheduled to go to Fort Yukon, Alaska and the date they had set for their wedding was after he would be leaving for Fort Yukon, so they eloped. Gayle had put a deposit on a wedding gown and lost the deposit. Eric left Gayle in Othello for the year because Fort Yukon was an unaccompanied tour.

Gayle married Eric in 1960 so I didn't have her to support. Garf was 16 then and Eileen was 11.

When he came home they and their new son left for Sioux City Iowa where Eric was to be stationed at the SAGE group there. They didn't have much money and the old car wasn't too reliable. They had an old Chevrolet which Eric kept running but I told Eric he could use the remaining gas in our storage drum. I couldn't help with money as my funds were low. We didn't know it but the gas had condensation in it and it fouled up their car so they had a terrible time getting it to run well enough to get to Sioux City. I sure hated to see them go. We missed baby Eric too. They had baby Eric and all their things in the car.

Eileen flew out to Sioux City to visit Gayle. She was 14 years old and excited to be flying there. She enjoyed this trip as she could be with Gayle and little Eric W. One day Eric W. got into a can of vegetable shortening and smeared it all over his body. He was crawling all over the place so Gayle had to move things in her cabinets so that Eric W. couldn't get into any further disasters.

While Eileen was in Iowa with Gayle there was a tornado. They were taking Eric W. for a stroll when the sirens began to fill the air with their sounds. It alerted Gayle so the 2 girls hurried home. The tornado passed close to where Gayle lived.

Eileen's trip home was very unpleasant. The plane flew thru an electric storm that caused Eileen a lot of anguish. The stewardess and passengers tried to reassure her that they would all be okay. She was crying and very distraught. Eileen doesn't enjoy traveling by plane. This experience has never left her.

Both Gayle and Eileen fear plane travel while Garf loves it and he took lessons so he could fly. I'll always remember the day he took us for a trip all over the Columbia Basin. He flew solo down to Portland Oregon at night for part of his training.

I was still going to summer school at Central Washington University so Garf and Eileen had to survive without me. I came home weekends to help out. Garf and I made root beer and I would cook up some food for them. I made arrangements with Ed Emery at his grocery store to let Garf and Eileen charge any food they needed. It was very hard for them as they were responsible for everything now that Gayle was gone.

Central Washington State College

Ellensburg, Washington

The Trustees of Central Washington State College at Ellensburg by virtue of the authority vested in them by the State of Washington and upon the recommendation of the President and Faculty have conferred upon

Irene F. Ivory

the degree of

Bachelor of Arts in Education

With all the rights, privileges and honors pertaining thereto.

In Testimony Thereof, we have subscribed our names, confirmed by the seal of the College on this twenty-first day of August, nineteen hundred and sixty-four.

James E. Brooks
President of the College

J. H. Bouillon
Chairman of the Board of Trustees

Irene was the first person in her family to graduate from college.

I spent so much time going to college that I didn't have much time left to give the children. This really bothered me a lot. I tried to keep up some correspondence with Gayle and Eric and little Eric W. as they moved a lot for the military.

Garf and Eileen survived and were helpful to me in a thousand ways. Garf also did custom farm work for many of our neighbors during this time.

Garf graduated from Othello High School and then attended Big Bend Community College in Pasco where he studied electronics. He also won about 52 trophies for his drag racing.

Eileen met Frank Rodriguez and fell in love with him. She graduated from Othello High School with honors. She insisted on getting married to Frank.

She was 18 so I couldn't postpone her wishes. She went to Texas with Frank and his folks put on their wedding.

I finally finished my summer school so I had some spare time. Garf gave me some money so I could fly from Seattle to Alaska with Anne Sandar and Ruth Lundstrom for a Presbyterian Church sponsored trip. We boarded the Presbyterian Church owned boat at Fairbanks and cruised all through the Alaskan waters. We cooked meals and invited the local Eskimos to join us. When the cruise was finished we flew back to Seattle. It was a very exciting and pleasure filled trip for me. Garf had really encouraged me to go.

Garf was alone now so his looking for someone special was important. He met several girls and in the end he started dating Maxine Gilbert. I think she was still in high school but that didn't stop Garf's pursuit of her. The fall after Maxine graduated from Othello High School, Garf and Maxine were married and lived in the farm house until I sold the farm to Mr. Vickery.

I bought a small home on Larch Street in Othello for $9000. It had 2 bedrooms and Garf and Maxine lived there next. Garf found a pre built home and bought it and put it on a farm he had purchased so I moved from Mom's garage into the little house and stayed there for quite some time.

During these years I took a couple of trips to Hawaii to see Gayle and Eric as they had moved a few times. They had Kama while they were back in Othello for a time and their family was complete. Eric had been stationed in Mt. Home, Idaho and finished his time with the Air Force. I had visited several times there. Then Eric joined the US Navy and went to Hunters Point to go thru his training for the Navy there. I also took the train to San Diego to see Gayle and the children while Eric was on the air craft carrier to cheer them up. He had been stationed in San Diego on the USS Constellation for a tour in Viet Nam. They next went to Hawaii to Kunia Facility there.

I missed having Eileen home when she married Frank and moved to Texas. Her welfare was always on my mind.

Bert fell one night in 1968 and hit his head on the bird cages. We had to get him to the hospital. I think he had a slight stroke. He stayed in the hospital for 10 days and that was all they could keep him. We took him to the Tri-cities and put him in a nursing home where he died about a month later on February 16, 1969. I always felt bad about leaving Bert there. We did visit him every week. I was working and couldn't keep him in his home as Mom wasn't able to care for him. I moved to Mom's and Bert's farm and lived in the garage when Bert died so I could sleep there for Mom's sake. I took care of her for about a year and then we moved her to Eureka, California to a retirement home there. That is where she wanted to go. She lived there for a year and half and passed away there on April 1, 1972.

Mom gave Cornell a quick claim deed to her property so I had to move anyway. I moved into my little house in town on Larch Street and lived there until I built my home on Juniper street. I wanted a bigger house so my children and grandchildren could come and stay for a visit.

Lucille and Bill had purchased a home in town that Earl Cooper had built and I liked it so that was the reason I hired Earl Cooper and his son as contractors to build mine. It was the last house that Earl built. He was coming home from the Tri-cities one day and had been drinking too much. He had an accident on a lonely county road and got stuck in a ditch full of water. He couldn't get out so he started walking toward a farm house light that he could see. It was winter and freezing cold weather. He never got to the farm house and he was found frozen to death.

The house on E. Juniper street cost me $34,000 to build. Garf and Gayle helped me buy materials for my new home. I bought all the materials for the house. I found the carpet, light fixtures, bathroom chest, and other things when I went to Bellingham to visit Gayle and her family. Garf found a good buy on the roof shakes from a man in Idaho that he knew. I did all the staining of the woodwork, cabinets, and doors. This home was my first complete home with carpets and I gloried in having nice soft carpet to walk barefoot on—and that is just what I did. I walked all over and through each room. It was a delicious feeling.

This had been my big retirement project. I have lived in this house since the fall of 1976 and enjoyed it all so much. I finally had room enough for my children and grandchildren to visit and stay awhile and they have all come to visit me many times.

I cooked special dinners for Thanksgiving and Christmas with a birthday dinner thrown in for Lucille. I tried to entertain more. I had a house warming for all my teacher friends so they could see my new home. I have grown old in one place.

I planted a garden each year and froze the produce to use. I made jellies and jams for the family. I raised flowers and gave them away to the churches when they needed extra flowers. The cemetery was made more colorful as we always took some flowers there for Memorial Day. People would often stop and tell me how beautiful my yard was.

Another project that I had after retirement was raising cantaloupes with Gayle. It turned out poorly because the soil wasn't suitable for them. Garf loaned us a strip of his farm for raising the cantaloupe. We didn't make any money but we chalked it up to a learning experience.

Retirement can be fun and I had my share of that.

I flew to Hawaii to visit with Gayle and Eric and family. I did this two different summers after I graduated from Central Washington State College. I had a delightful time at each visit. I would take them corn on the cob packed in one suitcase. It kept well as I left the husks on and wrapped each ear with cellophane. During my last trip to Hawaii the customs decided to inspect the luggage coming in as they had done for luggage going out of Hawaii. The attendant wanted me to open my suit cases and if I did we wouldn't have any corn. I put up quite a discussion with him and finally convinced him to let me pass through without an inspection. I think I had extreme fatigue and didn't feel well so he just let me go.

My summers in my new home were blessed with the presence of my grandson, Eric Wendl. I enjoyed having him so much. Garf hired Eric W. to help him in the summer to irrigate and help on his land. Kama only got to stay with me once.

I joined Delta Kappa Gamma which kept me busy. Delta Kappa Gamma is a teachers sorority that promotes the positives about teaching and offers scholarships to young women who want to be teachers. I was a part of many committees for our group.

Eric left the service after 13 years and moved to Kent Washington to work for Heath Techna as an assistant manager so I went to see them there. When Heath Techna downsized because of the Boeing lay offs, Eric lost his job there and decided to go ahead and go back in the Navy and finish out his time.

He was stationed as a Navy Recruiter in Bellingham Washington so I took several trips up there as well.

I went to Texas with Eileen and Frank. I took my car and drove about half the way. Driving after dark was hard for me because the wild animals come out, especially the armadillos, and it was very hard to miss them and not run over them. I took them with me as they were living in Othello by this time. We went down into Mexico while we were on this trip. Frank's brother and sister-in-law went with us. We traveled all around that part of Mexico and saw the poor areas and elite areas. We went thru a glass factory and were treated like nobility and we found out that the people in the plant thought we were from Washington DC instead of Washington state. They offered us special prices on the glass pieces there.

All I want to do now that I am getting old is to enjoy my children, grandchildren, and great grandchildren. I really love having them come to visit with me and they take me to their homes too so I can soak up their loving ways. I wish I could see them all more often. I realize that they have their families and are building their family memories as I did.

I am living alone as I have done for a long time. I don't drive anymore so I am not doing much. Just putting around in the garden and count my blessings when the family stops by to see how "Grandma Great" is. They lend a helping hand to things that I can't do.

I reminisce about old family memories, reunions, birthdays, friends and trips. I have stored up many precious moments to keep my tired old brain humming. Many of my old friends have passed on or moved away from Othello. There are so few left that it makes me sad to think about them. When we moved to Othello in 1952, there was only sage brush, tumble weeds and dust. The irrigation came and we soon had green fields. Many people planted trees for shade as the climate is dry and hot. We had gravel streets and very few stores to shop in. Othello has grown and changed as has the rest of America.

I know I have left a lot of exciting things out of my story. I will leave the rest up to my children. They can add parts to this story of an old lady who has been blessed with lots of understanding and love.

REUNION OF 2001

Reunion of 2001—Irene Paddock Ivory surrounded by most of her living family.

L—R front row: Aaron Ivory Strom, Kayla Jolene Szendre, Olivia Rose Szendre, Jayda Alexus Harmon, Eli Strom Montermini, Addison Sage Ivory, Briar Gary Ivory
L—R second row: Nicole Bea Strom, Chad David Montermini, Kama Gaile Strom Montermini, Rand Erick Montermini, Jana Rasmussen Ivory
L—R second 1/2 row: David R. Montermini and Gary Royal Ivory
L—R third row: Eric G. Strom, R. Garf Ivory, Irene Paddock Ivory, Gayle Ivory Strom, Eileen F. Ivory, Beth Kinne Strom, Erik M. Strom just in front of Beth, Eric W. Strom
L—R 4th row: Cliff Harmon, Joyce Goggin Harmon, Ray Leonard, Alice Ann Flint Leonard, Maxine Gilbert Ivory, Jolene Ivory Szendre, Darren Szendre, Ryan Garf Ivory holding Jacob Ryan Ivory, Christy Norton Ivory, Dana Rodriguez Deeter, Billie Jo Kendall Deeter
Missing are: Kjristi, Erika, Josh Harmon and Tyson Deeter

EPILOGUE

August 18, 2001

Mom and I just returned from our 21st trip to Eureka in 22 years. Almost every year she has told me it will be her last trip there (and all of us who have heard that just sort of laugh about it and know better). Each time we would go, Mom would speak of different memories and places and I would tell her that I couldn't remember them all and that she should write them down for us. About 6 years into our tradition of going to Eureka, Mom started her writing and this book is the result.

As a part of these trips, we almost always took side trips along the way. This time one side trip was to our old home in Grants Pass. We drove right into the driveway and up to the house and I got out and knocked on the door and a young teenage boy answered and I told him about helping with making the rock walls that are still there and asked him if the picture window was still there. The owners previous to he and his family had added on a dining room and garage. He invited me inside (I am sure when his parents found out, they were mortified) so I took a quick look and the windows were still there. The ditch that Eileen fell into when she was about 3 is still out front and runs by there. The floor is now carpet over the maple floors that Mom spoke about.

I drove us by the Fruitdale School which looks like it is still in use.

Our goal has always been to spend time with family and friends and we see almost everyone of family that lives in Eureka. We would go get Uncle

Sterl each day so that he could go everywhere with us. He is now 91 years old and Mom is 89. They have nearly a century of times shared from the days alone at the Paddock Place at Kneeland and through this visit there.

This year the first day was spent with Lester and Ester Gregory at Grandma Loena's place where Mom spent time living with her grandmother (Loena Lasell Paddock) and Lester when she was a teenager. Lori Riese and family had a barbeque for us the next day. We went by Hontoon Street where Mom and Uncle Sterl remember living for awhile as well. Drove by the Sunset Memorial Cemetery where Garfield is buried. We went by the Carson Mansion and The Eureka Inn. The last day we drove to Kneeland and down into the old Paddock property where I took a picture of the rock where the kids played when they were young. Visited with Donnavie and Billy and Candace at their homes. Sharon cooked dinner for all of us and we enjoyed everyone. Watched the deer play down the hill and said goodbye to Kneeland for this time. The last thing we did was to drive by The Bon Boniere where Mom got her strawberry and chocolate ice cream cone. It was the last thing on the list of things Mom had wanted to do and it was still open at 9pm at night so we were both happy about that. Mom used to go there as a teenager from time to time to get her homemade ice cream cones and it is a good memory for her.

Other years we have visited the Iaqua Cemetery, Sunset Memorial and Myrtle Grove Cemetery where many or our ancestors are buried. We have gone into Trinidad where Mom remembers the whales and whaling boats. We have stopped by the ocean to just look and enjoy. One year Garf went with us and another year Eileen went with us.

I have been honored to have spent all these times with Mom there and have become quite enamored of the Eureka area. I always feel at home when I get there now and also feel a large nostalgia when we leave. I know the area where Aunt Cele's baby was buried and I know where the house burned down and I know where the school was ....and all of this and more is now part of my life. Perhaps one day I will write a continuation from here.

These are Mom's words—sometimes repeated and not always in perfect chronology but nonetheless—her story. I know there are more stories she left out. Right now this is what I have to offer—the compiling and printing of Mom's Story, "My Space On Earth" for her to present to her family. I have done this with great feeling and love.

Love and hugs to all, Gayle

SUMMER 2001 .....KNEELAND, CALIFORNIA

Sterling F. Paddock with rock in distance that the Paddock children played on when they were young. It is located on the old Paddock Farm.

AND ARCATA, CALIFORNIA

Irene Paddock Ivory and Sterling F. Paddock standing with their grandmother Loena's rose bush that has been there on her homestead for about 80 years.

NOTE..................

1-13-1998: My cousin Donna told me that a man named Erickson called Eureka looking for Sterling Paddock and he was doing genealogy. He wanted to know if Harry Chalberg had had a child about this time and if it was living. Donna's brother Billy told Mr. Erickson that the baby had been killed. Quite a coincidence after all these years. Mr. Erickson said it was what he had thought. He later contacted Mom (Irene Ivory) and said he was so sorry about what had happened because of his father. See his letter on page 155.

Letter from Richard Erickson to Irene Paddock Ivory regarding his father Harry Charlesburg who changed his name to Charles Erickson.

Hello Irene

I am sending all the obituaries of your family that were in the Eureka newspaper. I don't know if they contain any information that you are not aware of.

I started researching my roots about two years ago. When I started I knew very little about either side of the family. It seems as though all of my roots were pulled like weeds and scattered all over and left to die. I think it is a real pity that my ancestors didn't at least pass down some verbal information.

I want to express my thanks to you as you have been a great help in at least filling in some of the gaps. Above all I hope that recalling this terrible incident didn't cause you any discomfort.. If it did I most certainly apologize. Not all of my research has turned out bad. I traced my mother's ancestors back to Pennsylvania and found out that all branches of her family were devout Mennonites!! One branch arrived in this country in 1731 and I have found that there are thousands of descendants that descend from my 8th grandfather.

I think this picture was taken in 1920. Do you agree? I hope these obituaries will be of some help to your daughter. Thank you again and I wish you many more years of good health.

God Bless
Dick Erickson

3rd from left: Harry Charlesburg - picture taken about 1920

Descendants of Irene Florence Paddock

1-Irene Florence PADDOCK

+Royal Andrew IVORY, m: 14 Dec 1938, Reno, Washoe, NV

|--2-Gayle Irene IVORY

| +Eric Gerald STROM

| |--3-Eric Wendl STROM

| | +Carol Ann FOXLEY

| | |--4-Kjristi Ann STROM

| | | +Dan CARLTON

| | | |--5-Spri CARLTON

| | |--4-Erika Marie STROM

| | +Josh Lee William HARMON

| | |--5-Jayda Alexus HARMON

| | +Beth KINNE

| | |--4-Erik Michael STROM

| | |--4-Nicole B STROM

| | |--4-Aaron Ivory STROM

| |--3-Kama Gaile STROM

| +David Robert MONTERMINI

| |--4-Chad David MONTERMINI

| |--4-Rand Erick MONTERMINI

| |--4-Eli Strom MONTERMINI

|--2-Royal Garf IVORY

| +Maxine GILBERT

| |--3-Gary Royal IVORY

| | +Jana RASMUSSEN

| | |--4-Briar Gary IVORY

| | |--4-Addison Sage IVORY

| | |--4-Matea Ellie IVORY

| |--3-Ryan Garf IVORY

| | +Christy NORTON

| | |--4-Jacob Ryan IVORY

| | |--4-Katie June IVORY

| | |--4-Daniel Joseph IVORY

| |--3-Jolene Maxine IVORY

| +Darren SZENDRE

| |--4-Kayla Jolene SZENDRE

| |--4-Olivia Rose SZENDRE

| |--4-Brielle Irene SZENDRE

|--2-Eileen Florence IVORY

+Francisco Maldonado RODRIGUEZ

|--3-Dana Lowell DEETER

+Renee JENSON

|--4-Tyson DEETER

+Billie Jo KENDALL

+James Daniel ANDERSON

+Bill DEETER

+Bobby Lloyd JOHNSTON

My Space on Earth

My goal in writing this book was to celebrate the life of our mother.

The first paragraph of the epilogue on page 151 tells why I started this project and it was such a joy to get it completed before Mom died.

I haven't done a new epilogue but should as she died on October 23, 2003 at age 91 and 4 months. We all miss her.

She has another great great grandson that was born after the book was written and I need to add him to her list of descendants. She was so thrilled that the family continued to grow.

Her story, like so many of her generation, is fascinating. She told me many times to just think about the happenings that had come about in her lifetime. We who love genealogy do think about these things.

My next goal is to try and find someone who makes Hallmark Hall of Fame type movies to look at mom's story. I think it would make a great movie. This is of course a lofty goal for someone who has no clue where to start. (grin)

Thank you for taking a moment to look at my mom's story.

Gayle Ivory Strom

6-10-04

THANKS

I want to especially thank Mom for taking the time to write her memoirs because it took a great bit of persistence and thought and many hours of time. Each trip would bring some new memory. As we all know I feel that time is the most precious gift we have to give one another and this gift from Mom will last for generations to come.

There have been 2 computer gurus who helped me get through all the "stuff" it took to put this together. Eric G. Strom has been there when I say come and fix the computer or printer and he kept them working for me. Jerri McCoy spent many hours sitting beside me and donated that time using her expertise to guide me with the software help that I really needed. Kama Montermini volunteered her time and did the binding with me. One person can never do this type of project alone.

THE IMMIGRANT TRAIN

(This is from an English paper dated January 23, 1933, by Irene Paddock)

Told to Irene Paddock by her Grandmother Loena Roxana Lasell Paddock

THE IMMIGRANT TRAIN

When I was a little tad of six years, I lived with my father and mother on the great plain. It was in the fall of the year when my folks decided to come west. I hated to leave this home of ours, because you could look for miles and see nothing but the waving grass which looked like the great Pacific Ocean. Now and then you could see a herd of buffalo or wild horses, and hear the cackle of the prairie chicken. We sold our farm, stock and household furniture and prepared to leave for the west in view of a milder climate. At Christmas time we were ready to leave. It was fiercely cold and the snow was several feet deep, and as we had heard of California's mild climate and beautiful scenery we decided to migrate there. The morning after Christmas we went to the nearest station and bought tickets to travel on The Old Immigrant Train to San Francisco. In those days the travel was of hardships and privation. Each person had to furnish their own beds and foods, and they suffered from the cold as there was only one stove in a car for eight or ten families to cook their meals on. The water was very poor coming over the prairie and it was very hard on small children who had to have lots of fresh water and milk. Several places we were delayed and one place we were stopped by Indians who were begging for clothing and what ever the people could give them. They were dressed in blankets and skins. Some had moccasins and the squaws had the little papooses under their blankets to keep them warm. We were delayed in another place when the cars broke and went back down the mountain. No one was hurt and the cars did not run off the track, but we were delayed several hours. The car we were in and the engine were the only ones that did not run back. As I said before we left home the morning after Christmas, and reached Humboldt the sixth day of January. After we left the boat and reached our destination, we saw that there was a mild rain and the fields were green and wild flowers bloomed almost everywhere. That was fifty years ago and you can see that I am a old lady now.

Notes From Irene Paddock Ivory…

My great grandmother and great grandfather moved from South Dakota to Eureka California. They traveled on the first immigrant train to come west (about 1869). Several families lived in a box car to make their trip. Quilts were used to section off their sleeping quarters. All of the families used a pot-bellied stove for cooking their meager meals. Usually corn meal mush was served three times a day along with molasses or honey. Milk was hard to get but when the train stopped at depots they could buy it as well as other foods to supplement their diets. Grandma had put up several crocks of pork, some salted or in brine and some cooked and preserved in a crock of lard. When they wanted the meat, pork chops or sausage patties, they just dug them out of the fat with a fork and put them in a pan to heat up. The lard kept out the air and preserved the meat. Their only water came from several wooden barrels which were secured in a corner of the box car. It was replenished at the depots or water filling stations. Sometimes they ran out of water or it became warm and tasted badly. A toilet was built in one corner. It resembled an old "chick-sales" toilet (and out door privy) but the waste was directly put on the railroad tracks as they traveled along. My dad became very ill on this trip. He got a bad cold which turned into brain fever as it was called. He almost lost his life but with Grandma's and Grandpa's medical skills they saved him. This was brought on because of the extreme cold weather as they crossed over the high snow covered mountains. The cold seeped in through the cracks in the box car. The people put quilts and blankets round the sides of the car and on the floor in their sleeping areas which didn't leave many covers to put over them while sleeping. They kept the stove burning all night but with the wind howling through the cracks it didn't do much good. During the day they sat on wooden benches bundled up in quilts. This trip began late in the fall of the year so they were exposed to the cold weather. Several of the box cars came loose from the train and rolled back down a long hill. It took the train crew a day to get them back on the train as one had jumped off the track. This was a very frightening experience for these pioneers. Since this was the first trip of the Pioneer Train the pioneer immigrants experienced a lot of hardships. Here-to-fore all pioneers had traveled in covered wagons. The railroad people learned that they would have to make the box cars more comfortable for their passengers if they were going to offer this service. Several people died on this trip from diseases caused by the extreme cold weather and poor nutrition. After improvements this then became a superior way of overland travel for the pioneers as it took only about 3 weeks to make this trip, a much shorter time than by horses and wagon.

My grandmother Paddock left Vermont when she was about 9 years old. She and her family traveled to Minnesota by wagon. She grew up to young womanhood in Minnesota. She met and married Grandpa Paddock at the end of the Civil War. He was 38 and she was 23. Their children, my Dad, Uncle Marion and Uncle Billy were born in Minnesota. The night my Uncle Billy was born, Grandpa went for a doctor but got caught in a blizzard and could not get back to their cabin that night. Grandpa had to walk 12 miles for the doctor and almost didn't get there because of a blizzard.

Grandma delivered Uncle Billy by herself. He was her second child. After he was born she bundled him up and crawled into bed with Uncle Marion on one side of her and the new baby on her other side. It was very cold in the cabin as she didn't have enough wood in the house to keep this fire burning. She was too weak to try and go outside in the raging blizzard to get wood so she piled quilts over them and her body heat helped keep the children warm. When she delivered her children, all 6 of them, she would kneel by the side of the bed with her arms and head resting on the side of the bed. This was the easiest position for her as she was so tiny, about 96 pounds then. Each birth was hard for her. Grandpa and the doctor made it back to the cabin the next afternoon.

After my Dad was born the family moved to South Dakota and lived in a one room cabin until they moved west on the immigrant train. The plains were so lonely that all Grandma could see was waving fields of buffalo grass or smoke curling from the chimney of a neighbor miles away—no trees—no flowers.

While living in the Dakotas, they couldn't find much wood to burn so Grandma and her 2 older children would pick up buffalo chips to use as fuel. The chips were dried out buffalo dung which was mainly straw as the rain washed out the other parts. The sun dried and leached the chips until they were a dark golden brown color. Grandma and her 3 little boys gathered chips every day all summer so that they could store them in their lean to for winter. She used some during the summer but relied more on the bundles of grass for cooking. They also gathered grass to store for winter fuel. This fuel didn't last long but it produced a quick good heat. It required constant stoking to keep it burning. Grandma would cut the buffalo or bunch grass, roll it into a round, log shape and tie it with some more grass trying to keep it compressed very tight. Grandpa would make wood when he could find a stand of willow trees or now and then a cottonwood tree but these were very scarce growing along stream banks or river bottoms. Grandma would also cut clumps of grass and tie them together with grass to be used for starting the fires. They also saved all the corn cobs for burning. The milk cows would eat the cut up stacks and leaves from the corn. Grandpa would use a scythe to cut enough feed for the cows for winter. He stored it in the lean-to beside the house which served as a shelter for the cows and also their supply of buffalo chips and wood or fuel for their stove. Since the temperatures dipped to 40 degrees or more below zero during the winter they experienced many cold days and nights using only enough fire fuel to cook their meals.

Grandpa was a good hunter so they had geese and ducks and rabbits to eat most of the year. They would hang the game from the eaves outside near their door and it would remain frozen all winter. Grandma saved the feathers from the fowl to make feather beds, and pillows. These were good for keeping them warm during the winter. They were so poor they had to sell their wagon and horses in order to buy the bare necessities for their first winter in South Dakota.

When spring came a neighbor plowed up a garden patch so they could plant their seeds. They built a cistern for water storage and collected rain water which ran off the roof into barrels. This wasn't much but Grandma liked it for washing her hair and their woolen clothes as it was very soft.

Washing clothes during the winter was a problem. They melted snow when they had it, and also icicles from the eaves. Grandma would get ice-nipped fingers when she hung the clothes outside even if she wore woolen mittens. The clothes would freeze almost as fast as she could hang them up. This did help to dry them some. When she brought them inside she could stand them up on the floor until they thawed out. The boys and Grandpa's pants looked so funny standing up without a body inside them.

Grandma would dry apples, pears and plums for the winter food supply. They usually got it from a traveling peddler or neighbor who had a few trees that bore fruit.

Grandpa worked for several farmers and got enough money to begin his blacksmith shop. After this he was better able to support his family. He was a very fine blacksmith. His work consisted of making horse shoes, wagon wheels, iron ladles and other things that could not be found in their small community. Much of his work was done for the pioneers moving west.

If he made a dollar a day it was considered very good wages for then.

That first Immigrant Train took them to San Francisco and there they boarded a tramp steamer vessel for Eureka California. They had around a thousand dollars with them which they had managed to save while in South Dakota. Grandpa could have bought most of the land for $1 an acre that now is Eureka California but Grandma didn't want to speculate so they bought some land at Trinidad, California.

When Grandmother was a little girl she loved to fish so she had her Dad bend a straight pin for a hook and worms were used for bait. There was a small creek near her home that always had many trout in its cool sparkling water. She would put her catch in her little apron and take them home for dinner. She was only five years old.

When Grandma was old enough she would be hired out to a family to help them with their housework and child care. This was a privilege as few families could afford to take on another mouth to feed and pay wages. Grandma did this so she could go on to school. She received her 9th year of schooling and a teaching certificate while living with this family. She scrubbed clothes, and the house, cooked, ironed clothes, and worked in the garden as well as tutor their children and attended school while doing all this.

She was so sad when her family moved from Vermont. All of her friends were left behind as well as the excitement of making maple sugar, riding in sleighs during the winter, quilting bees, and community get-to-gethers.

She loved the times when the whole family would make maple syrup and sugar. They drilled holes in the trees and put a spout in the hole so the sap from the maple tree could drip into buckets attached to the tree. They boiled the sap until it became thick. The children would take ladles of the hot syrup and pour it on the frozen crust of the snow. This cooled it and it became hard and something like taffy. They could eat it and enjoy their fruits of labor as the children had to help in the harvest. They put some of the syrup in crocks and the remainder was boiled some more until it crystallized and became sugary. Then they put it in cast iron muffin tins to form sugar cakes. These were stored in the cupboards near the fireplace to help keep it dry and hard.

Grandma especially enjoyed the winters for another reason. Sleigh riding. They would warm bricks in the fireplace for putting in the sleigh to keep their feet warm during their ride. Sometimes the snow was so deep they couldn't get out to go for a sleigh ride. Grandma told me that she could remember the snow covering the windows and blocking the doors. Her home had a door leading into a covered walkway which took them to the barn, so when the snow got too deep for them to get outside, they could get into the hrose stalls and cow barn through this walkway.

The animals had to be fed and the cow milked. They lived out in the country and great grandfather was a country doctor. Sometimes he had to wear snow shoes to visit his patients as the snow was too deep for the sleigh.

Another favorite activity of Grandma's was fishing in the spring of the year in a small brook near their home. Her dad would bend straight pins to make hooks which worked really well. They used worms as bait or bugs if a hatch was out. Grandma and her sisters always caught plenty of the small spotted trout to feed the family.

The year Lincoln became President, grandmother's father Zaro went to the village rally to wait for the results of the election. The village was several miles away so he had to ride his saddle horse. It was late in the afternoon when he got home. All of his family and some neighbors saw him as he rode through the field and trees. As he approached them he yelled out that Lincoln was president. Grandma's family and friends jumped and danced around yelling for Lincoln. Grandma climbed up on a stump of an old tree, took off her sun bonnet and waved it in the air, shouting loud hurrahs for Lincoln. She was about 6 years old then. They and their neighbors had their own little celebration for him. Grandma said it was very festive.

Her father was a doctor and was 25 years older than her mother. He got the urge to move west so uprooted his family and took off for greener pastures but they never found them. Great Grandfather Thomas Lasell delivered his wife when he was 25 years old. He told her mother that he would wait for her in a joking way and he did wait and marry her.

Great Grandfather and Grandmother Lasell had Uncle George, Silas, Marion, Mabel, Harriet, and Loena, my grandmother. Aunt Mabel was the youngest. Aunt Harriet died from breast cancer when she was a young woman. The doctor said it was from an injury. She had hurt her breast while pumping water from a well. The pump handle hit her breast and a big lump formed.

Note: This is the whole of the notes from Irene Paddock of her Grandmother Loena Lasell Paddock's story.

Ida Belle Fulmore
Baby Eileen
R. Garf Ivory
Eileen Florence Ivory
Irene Paddock Ivory
Gayle & Garf
Gayle Irene Ivory
CUFF
August 1947
Garf and Gayle

Charlotte Paddock Poyfaire William C. Paddock & Almira Paddock Scofield

1940
Loena Lasell Paddock

Sterling Paddock,
Irene Paddock,
W. Cornell Paddock,
Lucille Paddock,
Ida Belle Fulmore Paddoc

Claryse Bresheárs, Guy Bresheárs, Ruth Bresheárs, Irene Paddock and Louise Bresheárs

1934
Irene Florence Paddock

Irene Paddock, W. Cornell Paddock, Sterling Paddock, Garfield L. Paddock

Garfield L. Paddock

Sterling Paddock

Uncle Marion "Mary" Lasell

Zaro D. Lasell
Roxanna Moon Lund Lasell

Garfield L. Paddock